POLITICAL TREATISE

[Tractatus Politicus]

BENEDICT DE SPINOZA

Wherein is Demonstrated. How the Society in Which
Monarchical Dominion Finds Place, As Also That in Which the
Dominion is Aristocratic, Should be Ordered, so as not to
Lapse Into a Tyranny, but to Preserve Inviolate the Peace and
Freedom of the Citizens.

Including Chapter XX of

THEOLOGICO-POLITICAL TREATISE

[Tractatus Theologico-Politicus]

IN A FREE STATE EVERY MAN MAY THINK WHAT HE LIKES,
AND SAY WHAT HE THINKS.

Introduction by
R. H. M. ELWES.

Jorge Pinto Books, Inc.

JORGE
PINTO
BOOKS

Benedict Spinoza *Political Treatise.*

Edition Copyrights © Jorge Pinto Books Inc. 2018
This edition used the translation of Spinoza's work by R.H. M. Elwes,
published by George Routledge and Son Limited (London and New York)
in their collection: Sir John Lubbock's Hundred Books, (First Edition, 1884.
Second Edition, revised 1887.Reprinted, 1889, 1891.)

The text is formatted and corrected, including modernizing some words to
facilitate reading. We used several digital editions from the following sites
(PDF format files that we converted and fixed in the text)
http://www.gutenberg.org/files/989/989-h/989-h.htm
http://oll.libertyfund.org/titles/spinoza-the-chief-works-of-benedict-de-
spinoza-vol-1
Archive.org URL: https://archive.org/details/tractatustheolog00elweuoft

Copyright for the edición © Jorge Pinto Books Inc. 2018.

Cover and typography © Old &New | East & West Cultural Services, 2018.
Produced using iStudio Publisher for Apple Macintosh.

ISBN: 978-1-934978-67-2 | -1-934978-67-1

EEN
RECHTSINNIGE
THEOLOGANT,
OF
GODGELEERDE
STAATKUNDE.
BEHELSENDE
Eenige
REDENEERINGEN,

Met welke getoont word, dat de vriheid om te redenee-
ren niet alleen behoudens de Godsaligheid, en de
vrede des Gemeene-bests kan toegelaten, maar
ook dat deselve niet, dan te gelijk met de
Godsaligheid en vrede des Gemeene-
bests kan weggenomen worden.

1 Joh. 4: vers 13. *Hier door weten wy, dat wy in God blijven, en
God in ons, dat hy ons van sijn geest gegeven heeft.*

Uit het Latijn in 't Hollands vertaald.
En
Om sijn Voortreffelijkheid nu weer herdrukt.

Tot BREMEN,
By HANS JUNGEN von der Weyl/ 1694.

CONTENTS.

EDITOR'S NOTE

Born in Amsterdam in 1634, Benedict Spinoza continues to be one of the most admired thinkers. His work, including the *Ethics*, the *Tractatus Theologico Politicus* and the *Political Treatise* (first published in 1677, the year of Spinoza's death) that we present in this volume are widely read and the subject of philosophical, political, religious and psychological studies, not only by fellow philosophers but also by writers and poets. Among his admirers, Hegel declared that "to be a philosopher one must first be a Spinozist." Goethe wrote passionately about the influence of Spinoza in his life and work; "I, at last, chanced upon the Ethica of this man. To say exactly how much I gained from that work was due to Spinoza or to my reading of him would be impossible; enough that I found in him a sedative for my passions and that he appeared to me to open up a large and free outlook on the material and moral world."

Not only writers of the stature of Goethe but also famous poets became admirers and followers of Spinoza, particularly Lessing, Heine, Auerbach, Coleridge, Shelley, George Eliot and many more.

Robert Harvey Monro Elwes, a renowned XIX century English scholar and the English translator of Spinoza's works, in his Introduction to the *Tractatus Theologico Politicus*, (included in this book), wrote that these poets and intellectuals "not only admired him but studied him deeply. Shelley not only contemplated but began a translation of the *Tractatus Theologico-Politicus*, to be published with a preface by Lord Byron, but the project was cut short by his death."

Spinoza's ideas and remarkable talent continue to be the subject of numerous publications, including a recently published historical novel by Irvin D. Yalom, *The Spinoza Problem*. Explaining his motivation to write the book, Yalom wrote; "Spinoza, like Nietzsche and Schopenhauer, on whose lives and philosophy I have based two earlier novels, wrote much that is highly relevant to my field of psychiatry and psychotherapy—for example, that ideas, thoughts, and feelings are caused by previous experiences, that passions may be studied dispassionately, that understanding leads to transcendence—and I wished to celebrate his contributions through a novel of ideas."

Baruch Spinoza, a Sephardic of Portuguese or Spanish origin, became Benedict Spinoza after he was excommunicated by the Jewish community at a very early age in the Netherlands for his unorthodox ideas and the criticism of the sacred texts, ideas that became developed in his latter works.

We decided to publish the *Political Treatise*, Spinoza's last work written in 1677 which he did not complete. The *Political Treatise* is not as well known as it was published with the *Tractatus Theologico Politicus* which, it is mainly dedicated to biblical and religious questions. Like his *Ethics* contain critical interpretations of the Old Testament. For its political content and close relationship with the *Treatise* we included in the book the *Tractatus's* Chapter XX with the provocative title, "*In a Free State, Every Man May Think What He Likes, And Say What He Thinks.*"

For this publication, part of our series Rediscovered Books, we chose the translation of English writer and scholar R. H. M. Elwes published by George Routledge and Sons Limited (London and New York) in their collection: *Sir John Lubbock's Hundred Books*, (First Edition, 1884. Second Edition, revised, 1887. Reprinted, 1889, 1891.) We took the liberty to modernize some words to facilitate its comprehension.

The goal of our Rediscovered Books collection is to bring back classic books that are either out of print or difficult to find. Among these, we are proud to include the *Letters between Hermann Hesse and Thomas Mann* with an introduction of Pete Hamill, as well as the biographies of *Stendhal*, *Rousseau* and *Victor Hugo* by Matthew Josephson and two works of the English author Charles Morgan who in the 1930s was a bestseller author. In Spanish we included in the collection *Santa,* a famous novel by Federico Gamboa with a short essay by Cristina Pacheco, *El Delirio de Santa* and recently we added a series of classical Spanish authors from the XV to the XVII century such as *La Lozana Andaluza* by Francisco Delicado, *Cárcel de Amor* by Diego de San Pedro and *Laberinto de Fortuna* by Juan de Mena.

We believe that books are great learning tools and reading is at the core of self-educational projects. We live at a time where *"knowledge is power"*. The famous business philosopher Peter Drucker envisioned the rise of the "knowledge workers" a phrase he coined in *The Age of Discontinuity* ,published in 1969.

Italo Calvino states that a *"classic is a book which has never exhausted all it has to say to its readers"* (*Why Read the Classics?*). Following this idea, in this series we intend to bring back those classics that continue to be valuable and relevant in our modern world.

To read is a necessity in our changing societies. It is also an extraordinary pleasure. I am sure that reading the texts of Spinoza will add to the reader's knowledge and understanding of the complexities of the human condition.

———

Irvin D. Yalom. *The Spinoza Problem.* Basic Books. 2012

Peter Drucker. *The Age of Discontinuity: Guidelines to Our Changing Society.* New York: Harper & Row, 1969

Italo Calvino. *Why Read the Classics* Pantheon Books, 1986,

Introduction By R. H. M. Elwes.

It is acknowledged that the life of Spinoza was free from blame and pure and
immaculate as the life of his godly cousin, Jesus Christ. Like him, he suffered for
his doctrine, he wore the crown of thorns. Where a great spirit expresses his
memory is Golgotha. "-   --
HEINE. Ed.Tr.

A VERY few years ago the writings of Spinoza were. almost unknown in
this country. The only authorities to which the English reader could be
referred were the brilliant essays of Mr. Froude /1 and Mr. Matthew
Arnold, the graphic but somewhat misleading sketch in LeWes's "History
of Philosophy," and the unsatisfactory volume of Dr. R. Willis./3 But in
1880 Mr. Pollock brought out his most valuable " Spinoza, his Life and
Philosophy," /4 likely long to remain the standard work on the subject;
Dr. Martineau has followed with a sympathetic and gracefully written
"Study of Spinoza; " Professor Knight has edited a volume of Spinozistic
Essays by Continental Philosophers; Auerbach's biographical novel/5
has been translated, and many writers have made contributions to the
subject in magazines and reviews.

At first sight this stir of tardy recognition may seem less surprising than
the preceding apathy, for history can show figures more remarkable
than the solitary thinker of Amsterdam. But the causes which kept
Spinoza in comparative obscurity are not very far to seek. Personally he
shrank with almost womanly sensitiveness from anything like notoriety:
his chief work was withheld till after his death, and then published
anonymously; his treatise on Religion was also put forth in secret, and
he disclaims with evident sincerity all desire to found a school, or give
his name to a sect.

Again the form in which his principal work is cast is such as to repel those
dilettante readers, whose suffrage is necessary for a widely-extended
reputation; none but genuine students would care to grapple with the
serried array of definitions, axioms, and propositions, of which the

Ethics is composed, while the display of geometric accuracy flatters the careless into supposing, that the whole structure is interdependent, and that, when a single breach has been effected, the entire fabric has been demolished.

The matter, no less than the manner, of Spinoza's writings was such as to preclude popularity. He genuinely shocked his contemporaries. Advances in thought are tolerated in proportion as they respond to and, as it were, kindle into flame ideas which are already smoldering obscurely in many minds. A teacher may deepen, modify, transfigure what he finds, but he must not attempt radical reconstruction. In the seventeenth century all men's deepest convictions were inseparably bound up with anthropomorphic notions of the Deity; Spinoza, in attacking these latter and endeavoring to substitute the conception of eternal and necessary law, seemed to be striking at the very roots of moral order: hence with curious irony his works, which few read and still fewer understood, became associated with notions of monstrous impiety, and their author, who loved virtue with single-hearted and saintly devotion, was branded as a railer against God and a subverter of morality, whom it was a shame even to speak of. Those from whom juster views might have been expected swelled the popular cry. The Cartesians sought to confirm their own precarious reputation for orthodoxy by emphatic disavowals of their more daring associate. Leibnitz, who had known Spinoza personally, speaks of him, whether from jealousy or some more avowable motive, in tones of consistent depreciation.

The torrent of abuse, which poured forth from the theologians and their allies, served to overwhelm the ethical and metaphysical aspect of Spinoza's teaching. The philosopher was hidden behind the arch-heretic. Throughout almost the whole of the century following his death, he is spoken of in terms displaying complete misapprehension of his importance and scope. The grossly inaccurate account given by Bayle in the " *Dictionnaire Philosophique*" was accepted as sufficient. The only symptom of a following is found in the religious sect of Hattemists, which based some of its doctrines on an imperfect understanding of the so-called mystic passages in the *Ethics*. The first real recognition came from Lessing, who found in Spinoza a strength and solace he sought in vain elsewhere, though he never accepted the system as a whole. His conversation with Jacobi (1780), a diligent though hostile student of the *Ethics*, may be said to mark the beginning of a new epoch in the history of Spinozism. Attention once attracted was never again withdrawn, and received a powerful impulse from Goethe, who more than once confessed his indebtedness to the *Ethics*, which indeed is abundantly evident throughout his writings. Schleiermacher paid an eloquent tribute to "the holy, the rejected Spinoza." Novalis celebrated him as "the man intoxicated with Deity" (der Gottvertrunkene Mann), and Heine for once forgot to sneer, as he recounted his life. The brilliant novelist, Auerbach, has not only translated his complete works, but has also made his history the subject of a biographical romance. Among German philosophers Kant is, perhaps, the last, who shows no traces of Spinozism. Hegel has declared, that "to be a philosopher one must first be a Spinozist." In recent years a new impulse has been given to the study of the *Ethics* by their curious harmony with the last results of physiological research.

In France Spinoza has till lately been viewed as a disciple and perverter of Descartes. M. Emile Saisset prefixed to his translation of the philosopher's chief works a critical introduction written from this standpoint. Since the scientific study of philosophic systems has begun among the French, M. Paul Janet has written on Spinoza as a link in the chain of the history of thought; a new translation of his complete works has been started, and M. Renan has delivered a discourse on him at the bicentenary of his death celebrated at the Hague.

In Holland there has also been a revival of interest in the illustrious Dutch thinker. Professors Van Vloten and Land were mainly instrumental in procuring the erection of a statue to his memory, and are now engaged in a fine edition of his Works, of which the first volume has appeared./6 In England, as before said, the interest in Spinoza has till recently been slight. The controversialists of the eighteenth century, with the exception of Toland, passed him by as unworthy of serious study. The first recognition of his true character came probably from Germany through Coleridge. who in his desultory way expressed enthusiastic admiration, and recorded his opinion (in a pencil note to a passage in Schelling), that the *Ethics*, the *Novum Organum*, and the Critique of Pure Reason were the three greatest works written since the introduction of Christianity. The influence of Spinoza has been traced by Mr. Pollock in Wordsworth, and it is on record. that Shelley not only contemplated but began a translation of the *Tractatus Theologico-Politicus*, to be published with a preface by Lord Byron, but the project was cut short by his death. It is said that George Eliot left behind her at her decease a MS. translation of the *Ethics*.

It may strike those who are strangers to Spinoza as curious, that, notwithstanding the severely abstract nature of his method, so many poets and imaginative writers should be found among his adherents. Lessing, Goethe, Heine, Auerbach, Coleridge, Shelley, George Eliot; most of these not only admired him, but studied him deeply. On closer approach the apparent anomaly vanishes. There is about Spinoza a power and a charm, which appeals strongly to the poetic sense. He seems to dwell among heights, which most men see only in far of momentary glimpses. The world of men is spread out before him, the workings of the human heart lie bared to his gaze, but he does not fall to weeping, or to laughter, or to reviling: his thoughts are ever with the eternal, and something of the beauty and calm of eternal things has passed into his teaching. If we may, as he himself was wont to do, interpret spiritually a Bible legend, we may say of him that, like Moses returning from Sinai, he bears in his presence the witness that he has held communion with the Most High.

The main authority for the facts of Spinoza's life is a short biography by Johannes Colerus /7 (Kohler), Lutheran pastor at the Hague, who occupied the lodgings formerly tenanted by the philosopher. The orthodox Christian felt a genuine abhorrence for the doctrines, which he regarded as atheistic, but was honest enough to recognize the stainless purity of their author's character. He sets forth what he has to say with a quaint directness in admirable keeping with the outward simplicity of the life he depicts.

Further authentic information is obtainable from passing notices in the works of Leibniz, and from Spinoza's published correspondence, though the editors of the latter have suppressed all that appeared to them of merely personal interest. There is also a biography attributed to Lucas, physician at the Hague (1712), but this is merely a confused panegyric, and is often at variance with more trustworthy records. Additional details may be gleaned from Bayle's hostile and inaccurate article in the " *Dictionnaire Philosophque*;" from S. Kortholt's preface to the second edition (1700) of his father's book *"De tribus impostoribus magnis:* " and, lastly, from the recollections of Colonel Stoupe (1673), an officer in the Swiss service, who had met the philosopher at Utrecht, but does not contribute much to our knowledge.

Baruch de Spinoza was born in Amsterdam Nov. 24, 1634. His parents were Portuguese, or possibly Spanish Jews, who had sought a refuge in the Netherlands from the rigors of the Inquisition in the Peninsula. Though nothing positive is known of them. they appear to have been in easy circumstances, and certainly bestowed on their only son—their other two children being girls—a thorough education according to the notions of their time and sect the Jewish High School, under the guidance of Morteira, a learned Talmudist, and possibly of the brilliant Manasseh Ben Israel, who afterwards (1655) was employed to petition from Cromwell the re-admission of the Jews to England, the young Spinoza was instructed in the learning of the Hebrews, the mysteries of the Talmud and the Cabbala, the text of the Old Testament, and the commentaries of Ibn Ezra and Maimonides. Readers of the Tractatus Theologico-Politicus will be able to appreciate the use made of this early training. Besides such severer studies, Spinoza was, in obedience to Rabbinical tradition, made acquainted with a manual trade, that of lens polish- ing, and gained a knowledge of French, Italian, and German; Spanish, Portuguese, and Hebrew were almost his native tongues, but curiously enough, as we learn from one of his lately discovered letters,/8 he wrote Dutch with difficulty. Latin was not included in the Jewish curriculum, being tainted with the suspicion of heterodoxy, but Spinoza, feeling probably that it was the key to much of the world's best knowledge, set himself to learn it;/9 first, with the aid of a German master, afterwards at the house of Francis Van den Ende, a physician. It is probably from the latter that he gained the sound knowledge of physical science, which so largely leavened his philosophy; and, no doubt, he at this time began the study of Descartes, whose reputation towered above the learned world of the period.

Colerus relates that Van den Ende had a daughter, Clara Maria, who instructed her father's pupils in Latin and music during his absence. "She was none of the most beautiful, but she had a great deal of wit," and as the story runs displayed her sagacity by rejecting the proffered love of Spinoza for the sake of his fellow-pupil Kerkering, who was able to enhance his attractions lay the gift of a costly pearl necklace. It is certain that Van den Ende's daughter and Kerkering were married in 1671, but the tradition of the previous love affair accords ill with ascertained dates.

Clara Maria was only seven years old when Spinoza left her father's house, and sixteen when he left the neighborhood.

Meanwhile the brilliant Jewish student was overtaken by that mental crisis, which has come over so many lesser men before and since. The creed of his fathers was found unequal to the strain of his own wider knowledge and changed spiritual needs. The Hebrew faith with its immemorial antiquity, its unbroken traditions, its myriads of martyrs, could appeal to an authority which no other religion has equalled, and Spinoza, as we know from a passage in one of his letters,/10 felt the claim to the full. We may he sure that the gentle and reserved youth was in no haste to obtrude his altered views, but the time arrived when they could no longer he with honesty concealed. The Jewish doctors were exasperated at the defection of their most promising pupil, and endeavored to retain him in their communion by the offer of a yearly pension of 1,000 florins. Such overtures were of course rejected. Sterner measures were then resorted to. It is even related, on excellent authority, that Spinoza's life was attempted as he was coming out of the Portuguese synagogue. Be this as it may, he fled from Amsterdam, and was (1050) formally excommunicated and anathematized according to the rites of the Jewish church.

Thus isolated from his kindred, he sought more congenial society among the dissenting community of Collegians, a body of men who without priests or set forms of worship carried out the precepts of simple piety. He passed some time in the house of one of that body, not far from Amsterdam, on the Ouwerkerk road, and in 1660 or the following year removed with his friend to the headquarters of the sect at Rhijnsburg, near Leyden, where the memory of his sojourn is still preserved in the name "Spinoza Lane." His separation from Judaism was marked by his substituting for his name Baruch the Latin equivalent Benedict, but he never received baptism or formally joined any Christian sect. Only once again does his family come into the record of his life. On the death of his father, his sisters endeavored to deprive him of his share of the inheritance on the ground that he was an outcast and heretic. Spinoza resisted their claim by law, but on gaining his suit yielded up to them all they had demanded except one bed.

Skill in polishing lenses gave him sufficient money for his scanty needs, and he acquired a reputation as an optician before he became known as a philosopher. It was in this capacity that he was consulted by Leibniz./11 His only contribution to the science was a short treatise on the rainbow, printed posthumously in 1687. This was long regarded as lost, but has, in our own time, been recovered and reprinted by Dr. Van Vloten.

Spinoza also drew, for amusement, portraits of his friends with ink or charcoal. Colerus possessed "a whole book of such draughts, amongst which there were some heads of several considerable persons, who were known to him, or had occasion to visit him," and also a portrait of the philosopher himself in the costume of Masaniello.

So remarkable a man could hardly remain obscure, and we have no reason to suppose that Spinoza shrank from social intercourse. Though in the last years of his life his habits were somewhat solitary, this may be set down to failing health, poverty, and the pressure of uncompleted work. He was never a professed ascetic, and probably, in the earlier years of his separation from Judaism, was the centre of an admiringly and affectionate circle of friends. In his letters he frequently states that visitors leave him no time for correspondence, and the tone, in which he was ad- dressed by comparative strangers, shows that he enjoyed considerable reputation and respect. Before the appearance of the *Tractatus Tlieologico-Politieus*, he had published nothing which could shock the susceptibilities of Christians, and he was known to be a complete master of Cartesianism, then regarded as the consummation and crown of learning. It is recorded that a society of young men used to hold meetings in Amsterdam for the discussion of philosophical problems, and that Spinoza contributed papers as material for their debates./12 Possibly the MS. treatise *"On God, Man, and his Blessedness,"* which has been re-discovered in two Dutch copies during our own time, may be referred to this period. It is of no philosophic value compared with the *Ethics*, but is interesting historically as throwing light on the growth of Spinoza's mind and his early relations to Cartesianism.

Oblivion has long since settled down over this little band of questioners, but a touching record has been preserved of one of their number, Simon de Vries, who figures in Spinoza's correspondence. He had often, we are told, wished to bestow gifts of money on his friend and master, but these had always been declined. During the illness which preceded his early death, he expressed a desire in make the philosopher his heir. This again was declined, and he was prevailed on by Spinoza to reduce the bequest to a small annuity, and to leave the bulk of his property to his family. When he had passed away his brother fixed the pension at 500 florins, but Spinoza declared the sum excessive, and refused to accept more than 300 florins, which were punctually paid him till his death.

Besides this instruction by correspondence, for which he seems to have demanded no payment ("mischief," as one of his biographers puts it, " could be had from him for nothing"), Spinoza at least in one instance received into his house a private pupil,/13 generally identified with one Albert Burgh, who became a convert to Rome in 1675, and took that occasion to admonish his ex-tutor in a strain of contemptuous pity./14 Probably to this youth were dictated "*The principles of Cartesianism geometrically demonstrated*," which Spinoza was induced by his friends to publish, with the addition of some metaphysical reflections, in 1663./15 Lewis Meyer, a physician of Amsterdam, and one of Spinoza's intimates, saw the book through the press, and supplied a preface. Its author does not appear to have attached any importance to the treatise, which he regarded merely as likely to pave the way for the reception of more original work. It is interesting as an example of the method afterwards employed in the *Ethics*, used to support propositions not accepted by their expounder. It.also shows that Spinoza thoroughly understood the system he rejected.

In the same year the philosopher removed from Rhijnsburg to Voorburg, a suburb of the Hague, and in 1670 to the Hague itself, where he lived till his death in 1677, lodging first in the house (afterwards tenanted by Colerus) of the widow Van Velden, and subsequently with Van der Spijk, a painter. He was very likely led to leave Rhijusburg by his increasing reputation and a desire for educated society. By this time he was well known in Holland, and counted among his friends, John de Witt, who is said to have consulted him on afiairs of state. Nor was his fame confined to his native country. Henry Oldenburg, the first secretary of the newly-established Royal Society of England, had visited him at Rhijnsburg, introduced possibly by Huyghens, and had invited him to carry on a correspondence,/16 in terms of affectionate intimacy. Oldenburg was rather active-minded than able, never really understood or sympathized with Spinoza's standpoint, and was thoroughly shocked/17 at the appearance of the *Traetatus Theologico-Politieus*, but he was the intimate friend of Robert Boyle, and kept his correspondent acquainted with the progress of science in England. Later on (1671),

Leibniz consulted Spinoza on a question of practical optics,/18 and in 1676, Ludwig von Tschirnhausen, a Bohemian nobleman, known in the history of mathematical science, contributed some pertinent criticisms on the *Ethics*, then circulated in MS./19

Amusing testimonies to Spinoza's reputation are afforded by the volunteered effusions of Blyenbergh,/20 and the artless questionings of the believer in ghosts./21

In 1670, the *Tractatus Theologico-Politieus* was published anonymously, with the name of a fictitious printer at Hamburg. It naturally produced a storm of angry controversy. It was, in 1674, formally prohibited by the States-General, and, as a matter of course, was placed on the Index by the Romish Church. Perhaps few books have been more often "refuted," or less seriously damaged by the ordeal. Its author displayed his disinclination to disturb the faith of the unlearned by preventing during his lifetime the appearance of the book in the vernacular.

In 1672, men's thoughts were for a time diverted from theological controversy by the French invasion of the Netherlands, and the consequent outbreak of domestic faction. The shameful massacre of the brothers De Witt by an infatuated mob brought Spinoza into close and painful contact with the passions seething round him. For once his philosophic calm was broken: he was only by force prevented from rushing forth into the streets at the peril of his life, and proclaiming his abhorrence of the crime.

Shortly afterwards, when the headquarters of the French army were at Utrecht, Spinoza was sent for by the Prince de Condé, who wished to make his acquaintance. On his arrival at the camp, however, he found that the Prince was absent; and, after waiting a few days, returned home without having seen him. The philosopher's French entertainers held out hopes of a pension from Louis XIV., if a book were dedicated to that monarch; but these overtures were declined.

On his arrival at the Hague, Spinoza was exposed to considerable danger from the excited populace, who suspected him of being a spy. The calm, which had failed him on the murder of his friend, remained unruffled by the peril threatening himself. He told his landlord, who was in dread of the house being sacked, that, if the mob showed any signs of violence, he would go out and speak to them in person, though they should serve him as they had served the unhappy De Witts. "I am a good republican," he added, "and have never had any aim but the welfare and good of the State."

In 1673, Spinoza was offered by the Elector Palatine, Charles Lewis,/22 a professorship of philosophy at Heidelberg, but declined it,/23 on the plea that teaching would interfere with his original work, and that doctrinal restrictions, however slight, would prove irksome.

In the following year, the *Ethics* were finished and circulated in MS. among their author's friends. Spinoza made a journey to Amsterdam for the purpose of publishing them, but changed his intention on learning that they would probably meet with a stormy reception. Perhaps failing health strengthened his natural desire for peace, and considerations of personal renown never had any weight with him.

To this closing period belong the details as to Spinoza's manner of life collected by Colerus. They are best given in the biographer's simple words, as rendered in the contemporary English version: "It is scarce credible how sober and frugal he was. Not that he was reduced to so great a poverty, as not to be able to spend more, if he had been willing. He had friends enough, who offered him their purses, and all manner of assistance; but he was naturally very sober, and would be satisfied with little." His food apparently cost him but a few pence a day, and he drank hardly any wine. "He was often invited to eat with his friends, but chose rather to live upon what he had at home, though it were never so little, than to sit down to a good table at the expense of another man. . . . He was very careful to cast up his accounts every quarter; which he did, that he might spend neither more nor less than what he could spend every year. And he would say some-times to the people of the house, that he was like the serpent, who forms a circle with his tail in his mouth, to denote that he had nothing left at the year's end. He added, that he designed to lay up no more money than what would be necessary for him to have a decent burying. . . .

He was of a middle size; he had good features in his face, the skin somewhat black; black curled hair; long eye- brows, and of the same colour, so that one might easily know by his looks that he was descended from Portuguese Jews. . . . If he was very frugal in his way of living, his conversation was also very sweet and easy. He knew admirably well how to be master of his passions: he was never seen very melancholy, nor very merry. . . . He was besides very courteous and obliging. He would very often discourse with his landlady, especially when she lay in, and with the people of the house, when they happened to be sick or afflicted: he never failed, then, to comfort them, and exhort them to bear with patience those evils which God assigned to them as a lot. He put the children in mind of going often to church, and taught them to be obedient and dutiful to their parents. When the people of the house came from church, he would often ask them what they had learned, and what they remembered of the sermon. He had a great esteem for Dr. Cordes, my predecessor, who was a learned and good-natured man, and of an exemplary life, which gave occasion to Spinoza to praise him very often: nay, he went sometimes to hear him preach. . . . It happened one day that his landlady asked him whether he believed she could be saved in the religion she professed. He answered:"*Your religion is a very good one; you need not look for another, nor doubt that you may be saved in it, provided, whilst you apply yourself to piety, you live at the same time a peaceable and quiet life.*"

His amusements were very simple: talking on ordinary matters with the people of the house; smoking now and again a pipe of tobacco; watching the habits and quarrels of insects; making observations with a microscope —such were his pastimes in the hours which he could spare from his philosophy. But the greater part of his day was taken up with severe mental work in his own room. Sometimes he would become so absorbed, that he would remain alone for two or three days together, his meals being carried up to him.

Spinoza had never been robust, and had for more than twenty years been suffering from phthisis, a malady which, at any rate in those days, never allowed its victims to escape. The end came quite suddenly and quietly, in February, 1677. On Saturday, the 20th, after the landlord and his wife had returned from church, Spinoza spent some time with them in conversation, and smoked a pipe of tobacco, but went to bed early. Apparently, he had previously sent for his friend and physician, Lewis Meyer, who arrived on Sunday morning. On the 21st, Spinoza came down as usual, and partook of some food at the midday meal. In the afternoon, the physician stayed alone with his patient, the rest going to church. But when the landlord and his wife returned, they were startled with the news that the philosopher had expired about three o'clock. Lewis Meyer returned to Amsterdam that same evening.

Thus passed away all that was mortal of Spinoza. If we have read his character aright, his last hours were comforted with the thought, not so much that he had raised for himself an imperishable monument, as that he had pointed out to mankind a sure path to happiness and peace. Perhaps, with this glorious vision, there mingled the more tender feeling, tl1at, among the simple folk with whom he lived, his memory would for a few brief years be cherished with reverence and love.

The funeral took place on the 25th February, "being attended by many illustrious persons, and followed by six coaches." The estate left behind him by the philosopher was very scanty. Rebekah de Spinoza, sister of the deceased, put in a claim as his heir; but abandoned it on finding that, after the payment of expenses, little or nothing would remain.

The MSS., which were found in Spinoza's desk, were, in accordance with his wishes, forwarded to John Rieuwertz, a publisher of Amsterdam, and were that same year brought out by Lewis Meyer, and another of the philosopher's friends, under the title, "*B. D. S. Opera Posthuma.*" They consisted of the *Ethics*, a selection of letters, a compendium of Hebrew grammar, and two uncompleted treatises, one on politics, the other (styled "*An Essay on the Improvement of the Understanding*") on logical method. The last-named had been begun several years previously, but had apparently been added to from time to time. It develops some of the doctrines indicated in the Ethics, and serves in some sort as an introduction to the larger work.

In considering Spinoza's system of philosophy, it must not be forgotten that the problem of the universe seemed much simpler in his day, than it does in our own. Men had not then recognized, that knowledge is "a world whose margin fades for ever and for ever as we move." They believed that truth was something definite, which might be grasped by the aid of a clear head, diligence, and a sound method. Hence a tone of confidence breathed through their inquiries, which has since died away, and a completeness was aimed at, which is now seen to be un-attainable. But the products of human thought are often valuable in ways undreamt of by those who fashioned them, and long after their original use has become obsolete. A system, obviously inadequate and defective as a whole, may yet enshrine ideas which the world is the richer for possessing.

This distinction between the framework and the central thoughts is especially necessary in the study of Spinoza; for the form in which his work is cast would seem to lay stress on their interdependence. It has often been said, that the geometrical method was adopted, because it was believed to insure absolute freedom from error. But examination shows this to be a misconception. Spinoza, who had purged his mind of so many illusions, can hardly have succumbed to the notion, that his *Ethics* was a flawless mass of irrefragable truth. He adopted his method because he believed, that he thus reduced argument to its simplest terms, and laid himself least open to the seductions of rhetoric or passion. "It is the part of a wise man," he says, " not to bewail nor to deride, but to understand." Human nature obeys fixed laws no less than do the figures of geometry. "I will, therefore, write about human beings, as though I were concerned with lines, and planes, and solids."

As no system is entirely true, so also no system is entirely original. Each must in great measure be the recombination of elements supplied by its predecessors. Spinozism forms no exception to this rule; many of its leading conceptions may be traced in the writings of Jewish Rabbis and of Descartes.

The biography of the philosopher supplies us in some sort with the genesis of his system. His youth had been passed in the study of Hebrew learning, of metaphysical speculations on the nature of the Deity. He was then confronted with the scientific aspect of the world as revealed by Descartes. At first the two visions seemed antagonistic, but, as he gazed, their outlines blended and commingled, he found himself in the presence not of two, but of one; the universe unfolded itself to him as the necessary result of the Perfect and Eternal God.

Other influences, no doubt, played a part in shaping his convictions. We know, for instance, that he was a student of Bacon and of Hobbes, and almost certainly of Giordano Bruno, but these two elements, the Jewish and the Cartesian. are the main sources of his system, though it cannot properly be called the mere development of either. From Descartes, as Mr. Pollock points out, he derived his notions of physical science and his doctrine of the conservation of motion.

In the fragment on the *Improvement of the Understanding*, Spinoza sets forth the causes which prompted him to turn to philosophy./24 It is worthy of note that they are not speculative but practical. He did not seek, like Descartes, "to walk with certainty," but to find a happiness beyond the reach of change for himself and his fellowmen. With a fervor that reminds one of Christian fleeing from the City of Destruction, he dilates on the vanity of men's ordinary ambitions, riches, fame, and the pleasures of sense, and on the necessity of looking for some more worthy object for their desires. Such an object he finds in the knowledge of truth, as obtainable through clear and distinct ideas, bearing in themselves the evidence of their own veracity.

Spinoza conceived as a vast unity all existence actual and possible; indeed, between actual and possible he re- cognizes no distinction, for, if a thing does not exist, there must be some cause which prevents its existing, or in other Words renders it impossible. This unity he terms indifferently Substance or God, and the first part of the *Ethics* is devoted to expounding its nature.

Being the sum of existence, it is necessarily infinite (for there is nothing external to itself to make it finite), and it can be the cause of an infinite number of results. It must necessarily operate in absolute freedom, for there is nothing by which it can be controlled; but none the less necessarily it must operate in accordance with eternal and im- mutable laws, fulfilling the perfection of its own nature.

Substance consists in, or rather displays itself through an infinite number of Attributes, but of these only two, Extension and Thought, are knowable by us; therefore, the rest may be left out of account in our inquiries. These Attributes are not different things:, but different aspects of the same thing (Spinoza does not make it clear, whether the difference is intrinsic or due to the percipient) ; thus Extension and Thought are not parallel and interacting, but identical, and both acting in one order and connection. Hence all questions of the dependence of mind on body, or body on mind, are done away with at a stroke. Every manifestation of either is but a manifestation of the other, seen under a different aspect.

Attributes are again subdivided, or rather display themselves through an infinite number of Modes; some eternal and universal in respect of each Attribute (such as motion and the sum of all psychical facts); others having no eternal and necessary existence, but acting and reacting on one another in ceaseless flux, according to fixed and definite laws. These latter have been compared in relation to their Attributes to waves in relation to the sea; or again they may be likened to the myriad hues which play over the iridescent surface of a bubble; each is the necessary result of that which went before, and is the necessary pre- cursor of that which will come after; all are modifications of the underlying film. The phenomenal world is made up of an infinite number of these Modes. It is manifest that the Modes of one Attribute cannot be acted upon by the Modes of another Attribute, for each maybe expressed in terms of the other; within the limits of each Attribute the variation in the Modes follows an absolutely necessary order. When the first is given, the rest follow as inevitably, as from the nature of a triangle it follows, that its three angles are equal to two right angles. Nature is uniform, and no infringement of her laws is conceivable without a reduction to chaos.

Hence it follows, that a thing can only be called contingent in relation to our knowledge. To an infinite intelligence such a term Would be unmeaning.

Hence also it follows, that the world cannot have been created for any purpose other than that which fulfills by being what it is. To say that it has been created for the good of man, or for any similar end, is to indulge in grotesque anthropomorphism.

Among the Modes of thought may be reckoned the human mind, among the Modes of extension may be reckoned the human body; taken together they constitute the Mode man.

The nature of mind forms the subject of the second part of the *Ethics*. Man's mind is the idea of man's body, the consciousness of bodily states. Now bodily states are the result, not only of the body itself, but also of all things affecting the body; hence the human mind takes cognizance, not only of the human body, but also of the external world, in so far as it affects the human body. Its capacity for varied perceptions is in proportion to the body's capacity for receiving impressions.

The succession of ideas of bodily states cannot be arbitrarily controlled by the mind taken as a power apart, though the mind, as the aggregate of past states, may be a more or less important factor in the direction of its course. We can, in popular phrase, direct our thoughts at will, but the will, which we speak of as spontaneous, is really determined by laws as fixed and necessary, as those which regulate the properties of a triangle or a circle. The illusion of freedom, in the sense of uncaused volition, results from the fact, that men are conscious of their actions, but unconscious of the causes whereby those actions have been determined. The chain of causes becomes, so to speak, incandescent at a particular point, and men assume that only at that point does it start into existence. They ignore the links which still remain in obscurity.

If mind be simply the mirror of bodily states, how can we account for memory? When the mind has been affected by two things in close conjunction, the recurrence of one re-awakens into life the idea of the other. To take an illustration, mind is like a traveller revisiting his former home, for whom each feature of the landscape recalls associations of the past. From the interplay of associations are woven memory and imagination.

Ideas may be either adequate or inadequate, in other words either distinct or confused; both kinds are subject to the law of causation. Falsity is merely a negative conception. All adequate ideas are necessarily true, and bear in themselves the evidence of their own veracity. The mind accurately reflects existence, and if an idea be due to the mental association of two different factors, the joining, so to speak, may, with due care, be discerned. General notions and abstract terms arise from the incapacity of the mind to retain in completeness more than a certain number of mental images; it therefore groups together points of resemblance, and considers the abstractions thus formed as units.

There are three kinds of knowledge: opinion, rational knowledge, and intuitive knowledge. The first alone is the cause of error; the second consists in adequate ideas of particular properties of things, and in general notions; the third proceeds from an adequate idea of some attribute of God to the adequate knowledge of particular things.

The reason does not regard things as contingent, but as necessary, considering them under the form of eternity, as part. of the nature of God. The will has no existence apart from particular acts of volition, and since acts of volition are ideas, the will is identical with the understanding.

The third part of the *Ethics* is devoted to the consideration of the emotions.

In so far as it has adequate ideas, i.e., is purely rational, the mind may be said to be active; in so far as it has inadequate ideas, it is passive, and therefore subject to emotions.

Nothing can be destroyed from within, for all change must come from without. In other words, everything endeavors to persist in its own being. This endeavor must not be associated with the "struggle for existence" familiar to students of evolutionary theories, though the suggestion is tempting; it is simply the result of a thing being what it is. "Then it is spoken of in reference to the human mind only, it is equivalent to the will; in reference to the whole man, it may be called appetite. Appetite is thus identified with life; desire is defined as appetite, with consciousness thereof. All objects of our desire owe their choice worthiness simply to the fact that we desire them: we do not desire a thing, because it is intrinsically good, but we deem a thing good, because we desire it. Everything which adds to the bodily or mental powers of activity is pleasure; everything which detracts from them is pain. From these three fundamentals—desire, pleasure, pain —Spinoza deduces the entire list of human emotions. Love is pleasure, accompanied by the idea of an external cause; hatred is pain, accompanied by the idea of an external cause. Pleasure or pain may be excited by anything, incidentally, if not directly. There is no need to proceed further with the working out of the theory, but we may remark, in passing, the extraordinary fineness of perception and sureness of touch, with which it is accomplished; here, if nowhere else, Spinoza remains unsurpassed./25 Almost all the emotions arise from the passive condition of the mind, but there is also a pleasure arising from the mind's contemplation of its own power. This is the source of virtue, and is purely active.

In the fourth part of the *Ethics*, Spinoza treats of man. in so far as he is subject to the emotions, prefixing a few remarks on the meaning of the terms perfect and imperfect, good and evil. A thing can only be called perfect in reference to the known intention of its author. We style " good" that which we know with certainty to be useful to us: we style "evil" that which we know will hinder us in the attainment of good. By "useful," we mean that which will aid us to approach gradually the ideal we have set before ourselves. Man, being a part only of nature, must be subject to emotions, because he must encounter circumstances of which he is not the sole and sufficient cause. Emotion can only be conquered by another emotion stronger than itself, hence knowledge will only lift us above the sway of passions, in so far as it is itself "touched with emotion." Every man necessarily, and therefore rightly, seeks his own interest, which is thus identical with virtue; but his own interest does not lie in selfishness, for man is always in need of external help, and nothing is more useful to him than his fellowmen; hence individual well-being is best promoted by harmonious social effort. The reasonable man will desire nothing for himself, which he does not desire for other men; therefore he will be just, faithful, and honorable.

The code of morals worked out on these lines bears many resemblances to Stoicism, though it is improbable that Spinoza was consciously imitating. The doctrine that rational emotion, rather than pure reason, is necessary for subduing the evil passions, is entirely his own.

The means whereby man may gain mastery over his passions, are set forth in the first portion of the fifth part of the *Ethics*. They depend on the definition of passion as a confused idea. As soon as we form a clear and distinct idea of a passion, it changes its character, and ceases to be a passion. Now it is possible, with due care, to form a distinct idea of every bodily state; hence a true knowledge of the passions is the best remedy against them. While we contemplate the world as a necessary result of the perfect nature of God, a feeling of joy will arise in our hearts, accompanied by the idea of God as its cause. This is the intellectual love of God, which is the highest happiness man can know. It seeks for no special love from God in return, for such would imply a change in the nature of the Deity. It rises above all fear of change through envy or jealousy, and increases in proportion as it is seen to be participated in by our fellow-men.

The concluding propositions of the *Ethics* have given rise to more controversy than any other part of the system. Some critics have maintained that Spinoza is indulging in vague generalities without 'any definite meaning, others have supposed that the language is intentionally obscure. Others, again, see in them a doctrine of personal immortality, and, taking them in conjunction with the somewhat transcendental form of the expressions concerning the love of God, have claimed the author of the *Ethics* as a Mystic. All these suggestions are reductions to the absurd, the last not least so. Spinoza may have been not unwilling to show that his creed could be expressed in exalted language as well as the current theology, but his "intellectual love" has no more in common with the ecstatic enthusiasm of cloistered saints, than his " God" has in common with the Divinity of Romanist peasants, or his "eternity " with the paradise of Mahomet. But to return to the doctrine in dispute./26 "The human mind," says Spinoza, " cannot be wholly destroyed with the body, but somewhat of it remains, which is eternal." The eternity thus predicated cannot mean indefinite persistence in time, for eternity is not commensurable with time. It must mean some special kind of existence; it is, in fact, defined as a mode of thinking. Now, the mind consists of adequate and inadequate ideas; in so far as it is composed of the former, it is part of the infinite mind of God, which broods, as it were, over the extended universe as its expression in terms of thought. As such, it is necessarily eternal, and, since knowledge implies self-consciousness, it knows that it is so. Inadequate ideas will pass away with the body, because they are the result of conditions, which are merely temporary, and inseparably connected with the body, but adequate ideas will not pass away, inasmuch as they are part of the mind of the Eternal Knowledge of the third or intuitive kind is the source of our highest perfection and blessedness; even as it forms part of the infinite mind of God, so also does the joy with which it is accompanied—the intellectual love of God—form part of the infinite intellectual love, wherewith God regards Himself.

Spinoza concludes with the admonition, that morality rests on a basis quite independent of the acceptance of the mind's Eternity. Virtue is its own reward, and needs no other. This doctrine, which appears, as it were, perfunctorily in so many systems of morals, is by Spinoza insisted on with almost passionate earnestness; few things seem to have moved him to more scornful denial than the popular creed, that supernatural rewards and punishments are necessary as incentives to virtue. " I see in what mud this man sticks," he exclaims in answer to some such statement." He is one of those who would follow after his own lusts, if he were not restrained by the fear of hell. he abstains from evil actions and fulfills God's commands like a slave against his will, and for his bondage he expects to be rewarded by God with gifts far more to his taste than Divine love, and great in proportion to his original dislike of virtue."/27 Again, at the close of the *Ethics*, he draws an ironical picture of the pious coming before God at the Judgment, and looking to be endowed with incalculable blessings in recompense for the grievous burden of their piety. For him, who is truly wise, Blessedness is not the reward of virtue, but virtue itself. "And though the way thereto be steep, yet it may be found—all things excellent are as difficult, as they are rare."

Such, in rough outline, is the philosophy of Spinoza; few systems have been more variously interpreted. Its author has been reviled or exalted as Atheist, Pantheist, Monotheist, Materialist, Mystic, in fact, under almost every name in the philosophic vocabulary. But such off-hand classification is based on hasty reading of isolated passages, rather than on sound knowledge of the whole. We shall act more wisely, and more in the spirit of the master, if, as Professor Land advises, "we call him simply Spinoza, and endeavor to learn from himself what he sought and what he found."

The two remaining works, translated in these volumes, may be yet more briefly considered. They present no special difficulties, and are easily read in their entirety.

The *Tractatus Theologico-Politicus* is an eloquent plea for religious liberty. True religion is shown to consist in the practice of simple piety, and to be quite independent of philosophical speculations. The elaborate systems of dogmas framed by theologians are based on superstition, resulting from fear.

The Bible is examined by a method, which anticipates in great measure the procedure of modern rationalists, and the theory of its verbal inspiration is shown to be untenable. The Hebrew prophets were distinguished not by superior wisdom, but by superior virtue, and they set forth their higher moral ideals in language, which they thought would best commend it to the multitude whom they addressed. For anthropomorphic notions of the Deity as a heavenly King and Judge, who displays His power by miraculous interventions, is substituted the conception set forth in the *Ethics* of an Infinite Being, fulfilling in the uniformity of natural law the perfection of His own Nature. Men's thoughts cannot really be constrained by commands; therefore, it is wisest, so long as their actions conform to morality, to allow them absolute liberty to think what they like, and say what they think.

The *Political Treatise* was the latest work of Spinoza's life, and remains unfinished. Though it bears abundant evidence of the influence of Hobbes, it differs from him in several important points. The theory of sovereignty is the same in both writers, but Spinoza introduces considerable qualifications. Supreme power is ideally absolute, but its rights must, in practice, be limited by the endurance of its subjects. Thus governments are founded on the common consent, and for the convenience of the governed, who are, in the last resort, the arbiters of their continuance.

Spinoza, like Hobbes, peremptorily sets aside all claims of religious organizations to act independently of, or as superior to the civil power. Both reject as outside the sphere of practical politics the case of a special revelation to an individual. In all matters affecting conduct the State must be supreme.

It remains to say a few words about the present version. I alone am responsible for the contents of these volumes, with the exception of the *Political Treatise*, which has been translated for me by my friend Mr. A. H. Gosset, Fellow of New College, Oxford, who has also, in my absence from England, kindly seen the work through the press. I have throughout followed Bruder's text,/28 correcting a few obvious misprints. The additional letters given in Professor Van Vloten's Supplement,/29 have been inserted in their due order.

This may claim to be the first version/30 of Spinoza's works offered to the English reader; for, though Dr. R. Willis has gone over most of the ground before, he labored under the disadvantages of a very imperfect acquaintance with Latin, and very loose notions of accuracy. The *Tractatus Theologico-Politicus* had been previously translated in 1689. Mr. Pollock describes this early version as " pretty accurate, but of no great literary merit."

Whatever my own shortcomings, I have never consciously eluded a difficulty by a paraphrase. Clearness has throughout been aimed at in preference to elegance. Though the precise meaning of some of the philosophical terms (e.g. *idea*) varies in different passages, I have, as far as possible, given a uniform rendering, not venturing to attempt greater subtlety than I found. I have abstained from notes; for, if given on an adequate scale, they would have unduly swelled the bulk of the work. Moreover, excellent commentaries are readily accessible.

R. H. M. ELWES.

Notes:

1. " Short Studies in Great Subjects," first series, art. " Spinoza."

2. " Essays in Criticism," art. " Spinoza and the Bible."

3. "Benedict de Spinoza; his Life, Correspondence, and Ethics." 1870.

4. I take this early opportunity of recording my deep obligations to Mr. Pollock's book. I have made free use of it, together with Dr. Martineau's, in compiling this introduction. In the passages which Mr. Pollock has incidentally translated, I have been glad to be able to refer to the versions of so distinguished a scholar.

5. Spinoza: em Denkerlebeu." 1855. [Spinoza. (A Novel.) By Berthold Auerbach. New York:' Henry Holt & Co., 1882. i6mo, pp. 444. (Leisure Hour Series, No. 135.)]

6. " B. de Spinoza, Opera. 1." The Hague, 1882.

7 ' Originally written in Dutch (1706). Translated the same year into French and English, and afterwards (1723) into German. The English version is reprinted in Mr. Pollock's book as an appendix.

8. ' Letter XXXII. See vol. II.

9. A translator has special opportunities for observing the extent of Spinoza's knowledge of Latin. His sentences are grammatical and his meaning almost always clear. But his vocabulary is restricted; his style is wanting in flexibility, and seldom idiomatic; in fact, the niceties of scholarship are wanting. He reminds one of a clever workman who accomplishes much with simple tools.

10. Letter LXXIV.

11. Letters LL, LII.

12. Letters XXVl, XXVII, according to the corrected text of Dr. Van Vloten, herein adopted.

13. Letters XXVL, XXVII.

14. Letter LXXIII.

15. The full title is, *Renati des Cartes Principiorum partes I. et II. more geometrico demonstratee per Benedictum de Spinoza Amstelodamensem. Accesseruut. ejusdem cogitata metaphysica. Amsterdam, 1663."*

Same page[NE. John de Witt (24 September 1625 – 20 August 1672) was a key figure in Dutch politics a period of globalisation made the United Provinces a leading European power during the Dutch Golden Age.

As a republican he opposed the House of Orange-Nassau. He was also strongly liberal, preferring lesser power to the central government and more power to the regenten.

16. Letter 1. sqq.

17. But Tschirnhausen seems to have brought Oldenburg and Boyle to a better mind. Letter LXV.

18. Letter LL.

19. Letter LXL. sqq.

20. Letter XXXI. sqq.

21. Letter LV. sqq.

22. Letter LIII.

23. Letter LIV.

24. 1 These observations are not offered as a complete exposition of Spinozism, but merely as an indication of its general drift.

25. It may be worth while to cite the often-quoted testimony of the distinguished physiologist, Johannes Muller :—" With regard to the relations of the passions to one another apart from their physiological conditions, it is impossible to give any better account than that which Spinoza has laid down with unsurpassed mastery."—*Physiologie des Menschen*. ii, 543. He follows up this praise by quoting the propositions in question *in extenso*.

26. The explanation here indicated is based on that given by Mr. Pollock, " Spinoza," &c., ch. ix., to which the reader is referred for a masterly exposition of the question.

27. Letter XLIX.

28. "B. de Spinosa Opera quae Supersunt Omnia," ed. C. H. Bruder. *Leipzig (Tauchnitz)*, 1843.

29. "Ad B. D. S. Opera qae Supersunt Omnia Supplementum." Amsterdam, 1862.

BENEDICT DE SPINOZA'S POLITICAL TREATISE,

WHEREIN IS DEMONSTRATED. HOW THE SOCIETY IWHICH MONARCHICAL DOMINION FINDS PLACE, AS ALSO THAT IN WHICH THE DOMINION IS ARISTOCRATIC, SHOULD BE ORDERED, SO AS NOT TO LAPSE INTO A TYRANNY, BUT TO PRESERVE INVIOLATE THE PEACE AND FREEDOM OE THE CITIZENS.

[TRACTATUS POLITICUS.]

FROM THE EDITOR'S PREFACE TO THE POSTHUMOUS WORKS OF BENEDICT DE SPINOZA.

Our author composed the Political Treatise shortly before his death. Its reasonings are exact, its style clear. Abandoning the opinions of many political writers, he most firmly propounds therein his own judgment; and throughout draws his conclusions from his premisses. In the first five chapters, he treats of political science in general—in the sixth and seventh, of monarchy; in the eighth, ninth, and tenth, of aristocracy; lastly, the eleventh begins the subject of democratic government. But his untimely death was the reason that he did not finish this treatise, and that he did not deal with the subject of laws, nor with the various questions about politics, as may be seen from the following "Letter of the Author to a Friend, which may properly be prefixed to this Political Treatise, and serve it for a Preface :"——

" *Dear Friend,——~Your welcome letter was delivered to me yesterday. I heartily thank you for the kind interest you take in me. I would not miss this opportunity, were I not engaged in something, which I think more useful, and which, I believe, will please you more—that is, in preparing a Political Treatise, which I began some time since, upon your advice. Of this treatise, six chapters are already finished. The first contains a kind of introduction to the actual work; the second treats of natural right; the third, of the right of supreme authorities. In the fourth, I inquire, what political matters are subject to the direction of supreme authorities; in the fifth, what is the ultimate and highest end which a society can contemplate; and, in the sixth, how a monarchy should be ordered, so as not to lapse into a tyranny. I am at present writing the seventh chapter, wherein I make a regular demonstration of all the heads of my preceding sixth chapter, concerning the ordering of a well-regulated monarchy. I shall afterwards pass to the subjects of aristocratic and popular dominion, and, lastly, to that of laws and other particular questions about politics. And so, farewell."*

The author's aim appears clearly from this letter; but being hindered by illness, and snatched away by death, he was unable, as the reader will find for himself, to continue this work further than to the end of the subject of aristocracy.

CHAPTER I.

INTRODUCTION.

Philosophers conceive of the passions which harass us as vices into which men fall by their own fault, and, therefore, generally deride, bewail, or blame them, or execrate them, if they wish to seem unusually pious. And so they think they are doing something wonderful, and reaching the pinnacle of learning, when they are clever enough to bestow manifold praise on such human nature, as is nowhere to be found, and to make verbal attacks on that which, in fact, exists. For they conceive of men, not as they are, but as they themselves would like them to be. Whence it has come to pass that, instead of ethics, they have generally written satire, and that they have never conceived a theory of politics, which could be turned to use, but such as might be taken for a chimera, or might have been formed in Utopia, or in that golden age of the poets when, to be sure, there was least need of it. Accordingly, as in all sciences, which have a useful application, so especially in that of politics, theory is supposed to be at variance with practice; and no men are esteemed less fit to direct public affairs than theorists or philosophers.

2. But statesmen, on the other hand, are suspected of plotting against mankind, rather than consulting their interests, and are esteemed more crafty than learned. No doubt nature has taught them, that vices will exist, while men do. And so, while they study to anticipate human wickedness, and that by arts, which experience and long practice have taught, and which men generally use under the guidance more of fear than of reason, they

are thought to be enemies of religion, especially by divines, who believe that supreme authorities should handle public affairs in accordance with the same rules of piety, as bind a private individual. Yet there can be no doubt, that statesmen have written about politics far more happily than philosophers. For, as they had experience for their mistress, they taught nothing that was inconsistent with practice.

3. And, certainly, I am fully persuaded that experience has revealed all conceivable sorts of commonwealth, which are consistent with men's living in unity, and likewise the means by which the multitude may be guided or kept within fixed bounds. So that I do not believe that we can by meditation discover in this matter anything not yet tried and ascertained, which shall be consistent with experience or practice. For men are so situated, that they cannot live without some general law. But general laws and public affairs are ordained and managed by men of the utmost acuteness, or, if you like, of great cunning or craft. And so it is hardly credible, that we should be able to conceive of anything serviceable to a general society, that occasion or chance has not offered, or that men, intent upon their common affairs, and seeking their own safety, have not seen for themselves.

4. Therefore, on applying my mind to politics. I have resolved to demonstrate by a certain and undoubted course of argument, or to deduce from the very condition of human nature, not what is new and unheard of, but only such things as agree best with practice. And that I might investigate the subject-matter of this science with the same freedom of spirit as we generally use in mathematics, 1 have labored carefully, not to mock, lament, or

execrate, but to understand human actions; and to this end I have looked upon passions, such as love, hatred, anger, envy, ambition, pity, and the other perturbations of the mind, not in the light of vices of human nature, but as properties, just as pertinent to it, as are heat, cold, storm, thunder, and the like to the nature of the atmosphere, which phenomena, though inconvenient, are yet necessary, and have fixed causes, by means of which we endeavor to understand their nature, and the mind has just as much pleasure in viewing them aright, as in knowing such things as flatter the senses.

5. For this is certain, and we have proved its truth in our Ethics,/1 that men are of necessity liable to passions, and so constituted as to pity those who are ill, and envy those who are well off; and to be prone to vengeance more than to mercy: and moreover, that every individual wishes the rest to live after his own mind, and to approve what he approves, and reject what he rejects. And so it comes to pass, that, as all are equally eager to be first, they fall to strife, and do their utmost mutually to oppress one another; and he who comes out conqueror is more proud of the harm he has done to the other, than of the good he has done to himself. And although all are persuaded, that religion, on the contrary, teaches every man to love his neighbour as himself, that is to defend another's right just as much as his own, yet we showed that this persuasion has too little power over the passions. It avails, indeed, in the hour of death, when disease has subdued the very passions, and man lies inert, or in temples, where men hold no traffic, but least of all, where it is most needed, in the law-court or the palace. We showed too, that reason can, indeed, do much to

restrain and moderate the passions, but we saw at the same time. that the road, Which reason herself points out, is very steep;/2 so that such as persuade themselves, that the multitude or men distracted by politics can ever be induced to live according to the bare dictate of reason, must be dreaming of the poetic golden age, or of a stage-play.

6. A dominion then, whose well-being depends on any man's good faith, and whose affairs cannot be properly administered, unless those who are engaged in them will act honestly, will be very unstable. On the contrary, to insure its permanence, its public afiairs should be so ordered, that those who administer them, whether guided by reason or passion, cannot be led to act treacherously or basely. Nor does it matter to the security of a dominion, in what spirit men are led to rightly administer its affairs. For liberality of spirit, or courage, is a private virtue; but the virtue of a state is its security.

7. Lastly, inasmuch as all men, whether barbarous or civilized, everywhere frame customs, and form some kind of civil state, we must not, therefore, look to proofs of reason for the causes and natural bases of dominion, but derive them from the general nature or position of mankind, as I mean to do in the next chapter.

CHAPTER II.

OF NATURAL RIGHT.

In our Theologico-Political Treatise we have treated of natural and civil right,/3 and in our Ethics have explained the nature of wrongdoing, merit, justice, injustice,/4 and lastly, of human liberty./5 Yet, lest the readers of the present treatise should have to seek elsewhere those points, which especially concern it, I have determined to explain them here again, and give a deductive proof of them.

2. Any natural thing whatever can be just as well conceived, whether it exists or does not exist. As then the beginning of the existence of natural things cannot be inferred from their definition, so neither can their continuing to exist. For their ideal essence is the same, after they have begun to exist, as it was before they existed. As then their beginning to exist cannot be inferred from their essence, so neither can their continuing to exist; but they need the same power to enable them to go on existing, as to enable them to begin to exist. From which it follows, that the power, by which natural things exist, and therefore that by which they operate, can be no other than the eternal power of God itself. For were it another and a created power, it could not preserve itself, much less natural things, but it would itself, in order to continue to exist, have need of the same power which it needed to be created.

3. From this fact therefore, that is, that the power whereby natural things exist and operate is the very power of God itself, we easily understand what natural right is. For as God has a right to everything, and God's right is nothing else, but his very power, as far as the latter is considered to be absolutely free; it follows from this, that every natural thing has by nature as much right, as it has power to exist and operate; since the natural power of every natural thing, whereby it exists and operates, is nothing else but

the power of God, which is absolutely free.

4. And so by natural right I understand the very laws or rules of nature, in accordance with which everything takes place, in other words, the power of nature itself. And so the natural right of universal nature, and consequently of every individual thing, extends as far as its power: and accordingly, whatever any man does after the laws of his nature, he does by the highest natural right, and he has as much right over nature as he has power.

5. If then human nature had been so constituted, that men should live according to the mere dictate of reason, and attempt nothing inconsistent therewith, in that case natural right, considered as special to mankind, would be determined by the power of reason only. But men are more led by blind desire, than by reason: and therefore the natural power or right of human beings should be limited, not by reason, but by every appetite, whereby they are determined to action, or seek their own preservation. I, for my part, admit, that those desires, which arise not from reason, are not so much actions as passive affections of man. But as we are treating here of the universal power or right of nature, we cannot here recognize any distinction between desires, which are engendered in us by reason, and those which are engendered by other causes; since the latter, as much as the former, are effects of nature, and display the natural impulse, by which man strives to continue in existence. For man, be he learned or ignorant, is part of nature, and everything, by which any man is determined to action, ought to be referred to the power of nature, that is, to that power, as it is limited by the nature of this or that man. For man, whether guided by reason or mere desire, does nothing save in

accordance with the laws and rules of nature, that is, by natural right. (Section 4.)

6. But most people believe, that the ignorant rather disturb than follow the course of nature, and conceive of mankind in nature as of one dominion within another. For they maintain, that the human mind is produced by no natural causes, but created directly by God, and is so independent of other things, that it has an absolute power to determine itself, and make a right use of reason. Experience, however, teaches us but too well, that it is no more in our power to have a sound mind, than a sound body. Next, inasmuch as everything whatever, as far as in it lies, strives to preserve its own existence, we cannot at all doubt, that, were it as much in our power to live after the dictate of reason, as to be led by blind desire, all would be led by reason, and order their lives wisely; which is very far from being the case. For

" Each is attracted by his own delight." /6

Nor do divines remove this difficulty, at least not by deciding, that the cause of this want of power is a vice or sin in human nature, deriving its origin from our first parents' fall. For if it was even in the first man's power as much to stand as to fall, and he was in possession of his senses, and had his nature unimpaired, how could it be, that he fell in spite of his knowledge and foresight? But they say, that he was deceived by the devil. Who then was it, that deceived the devil himself? Who, I say, so maddened the very being that excelled all other created intelligences, that he wished to be greater than God? For was not his effort too, supposing him of sound mind, to preserve himself and his existence, as far as in him lay? Besides, how could it happen, that the first man himself, being in his senses, and master of his own will, should be led astray, and suffer himself to be taken mentally captive? For if he had the power to make a right use of reason, it was not possible for him to be deceived, for as far as in him lay, he of necessity strove to preserve his existence and his soundness of mind. But the hypothesis is, that he had this in his power; therefore he of necessity maintained his soundness of mind, and could not be deceived. But this from his history, is known to be false. And, accordingly, it must be admitted, that it was not in the' first man's power to make a right use of reason, but that, like us, he was subject to passions.

7. But that man, like other beings, as far as in him lies, strives to preserve his existence, no one can deny. For if any distinction could be conceived on this point, it must arise from man's having a free will. But the freer we conceived man to be, the more we should be forced to maintain, that he must of necessity preserve his existence and be in possession of his senses; as anyone will easily grant me, that does not confound liberty with contingency. For liberty is a virtue, or excellence. Whatever, therefore, convicts a man of weakness cannot be ascribed to his liberty. And so man can by no means be called free, because he is able not to exist or not to use his reason, but only in so far as he preserves the power of existing and operating according to the laws of human nature. The more, therefore, we consider man to be free, the less we can say, that he can neglect to use reason, or choose evil in preference to good; and, therefore, God, who exists in absolute liberty, also understands and operates of necessity, that is, exists,

understands, and operates according to the necessity of his own nature. For there is no doubt, that God operates by the same liberty whereby he exists. As then he exists by the necessity of his own nature, by the necessity of his own nature also he acts, that is, he acts with absolute liberty.

8. So we conclude, that it is not in the power of any man always to use his reason, and be at the highest pitch of human liberty, and yet that everyone always, as far as in him lies, strives to preserve his own existence; and that (since each has as much right as he has power) whatever anyone, be he learned or ignorant, attempts and does, he attempts and does by supreme natural right. From which it follows that the law and ordinance of nature, under which all men are born, and for the most part live, forbids nothing but what no one wishes or is able to do, and is not opposed to strifes, hatred, anger, treachery, or, in general, anything that appetite suggests. For the bounds of nature are not the laws of human reason, which do but pursue the true interest and preservation of mankind, but other infinite laws, which regard the eternal order of universal nature, whereof man is an atom; and according to the necessity of this order only are all individual beings determined in a fixed manner to exist and operate. Whenever, then, anything in nature seems to us ridiculous, absurd, or evil, it is because we have but a partial knowledge of things, and are in the main ignorant of the order and coherence of nature as a whole, and because we want everything to be arranged according to the dictate of our own reason; although, in fact, what our reason pronounces bad, is not bad as regards the order and laws of universal nature, but only as regards the laws of our own nature

taken separately.

9. Besides, it follows that everyone is so far rightfully dependent on another, as he is under that other's authority, and so far independent, as he is able to repel all violence, and avenge to his heart's content all damage done to him, and in general to live after his own mind.

10. He has another under his authority, who holds him bound, or has taken from him arms and means of defense or escape, or inspired him with fear, or so attached him to himself by past favor, that the man obliged would rather please his benefactor than himself, and live after his mind than after his own. He that has another under authority in the first or second of these ways, holds but his body, not his mind. But in the third or fourth way he has made dependent on himself as well the mind as the body of the other; yet only as long as the fear or hope lasts, for upon the removal of the feeling the other is left independent.

11. The judgment can be dependent on another, only as far as that other can deceive the mind; whence it follows that the mind is so far independent, as it uses reason aright. Nay, inasmuch as human power is to be reckoned less by physical vigor than by mental strength, it follows that those men are most independent whose reason is strongest, and who are most guided thereby. And so I am altogether for calling a man so far free, as he is led by reason; because so far he is determined to action by such causes, as can be adequately understood by his unassisted nature, although by these causes he be necessarily determined to action. For liberty, as we showed above (Sec. 7), does not take away the necessity of

acting, but supposes it.

12. The pledging of faith to any man, where one has but verbally promised to do this or that, which one might rightfully leave undone, or vice-versa, remains so long valid as the will of him that gave his word remains unchanged. For he that 11as authority to break faith has, in fact, bated nothing of his own right, but only made a present of words. If, then, 11e, being by natural right judge in his own case, comes to the conclusion, rightly or wrongly (for " to err is human"), that more harm than profit will come of his promise, by the judgement of his own mind he decides that the promise should be broken, and by natural right (Sec. 9) he will break the same.

13. If two come together and unite their strength, they have jointly more power, and consequently more right over nature than both of them separately, and the more there are that have so joined in alliance, the more right they all collectively will possess.

14. In so far as men are tormented by anger, envy, or any passion implying hatred, they are drawn asunder and made contrary one to another, and therefore are so much the more to be feared, as they are more powerful, crafty, and cunning than the other animals. And because men are in the highest degree liable to these passions (Chap. I, See. 5), therefore men are naturally enemies. For he is my greatest enemy, whom I must most fear and be on my guard against.

15. But inasmuch as (Sec. 6) in the state of nature each is so long independent, as he can guard against oppression by another, and it is in vain for one man alone to try and guard against all, it follows

hence that so long as the natural right of man is determined by the power of every individual, and belongs to everyone, so long it is a nonentity, existing in opinion rather than fact, as there is no assurance of making it good. And it is certain that the greater cause of fear every individual has, the less power, and consequently the less right, he possesses. To this most be added, that without mutual help men can hardly support life and cultivate the mind. And so our conclusion is, that that natural right, which is special to the human race, can hardly be conceived, except where men have general rights, and combine to defend the possession of the lands they inhabit and cultivate, to protect themselves, to repel all violence, and to live according to the general judgment of all; For (Sec. 13) the more there are that combine together, the more right they collectively possess. And if this is why the schoolmen want to call man a sociable animal—I mean because men in the state of nature can hardly be independent—I have nothing to say against them.

16. Where men have general rights, and are all guided, as it were, by one mind, it is certain (Sec. 18), that every individual has the less right the more the rest collectively exceed him in power; that is, he has, in fact, no right over nature but that which the common law allows him. But whatever he is ordered by the general consent, he is bound to execute, or may rightfully be compelled thereto (Sec. 4).

17. This right, which is determined by the power of a multitude, is generally called Dominion. And, speaking generally, he holds dominion, to whom are entrusted by common consent affairs of state—such as the laying down, interpretation, and abrogation of

laws, the fortification of cities, deciding on war and peace, &c. But if this charge belong to a council, composed of the general multitude, then the dominion is called a democracy; if the council be composed of certain chosen persons, then it is an aristocracy; and if, lastly, the care of afiairs of state and, consequently, the dominion rest with one man, then it has the name of monarchy.

18. From what we have proved in this chapter, it be- comes clear to us that, in the state of nature, wrong-doing is impossible; or, if anyone does wrong, it is to himself, not to another. For no one by the law of nature is bound to please another, unless he chooses, nor to hold anything to be good or evil, but what he himself, according to his own temperament, pronounces to be so; and, to speak generally, nothing is forbidden by the law of nature, except what is beyond everyone's power (Secs. 5 and 8). But wrong-doing is action, which cannot lawfully be committed. But if men by the ordinance of nature were bound to be led by reason, then all of necessity would be so led. For the ordinances of nature are the ordinances of God (Secs. 2, 3), Which God has instituted by the liberty, whereby he exists, and they follow, therefore, from the necessity of the divine nature (Sec. 7), and, consequently, are eternal, and cannot be broken. But men are chiefly guided by appetite, without reason; yet for all this they do not disturb the course of nature, but follow it of necessity. And, therefore, a man ignorant and weak of mind, is no more bound by natural law to order his life wisely, than a sick man is bound to be sound of body.

19. Therefore wrong-doing cannot be conceived of, it under dominion——that is, where, by the general right of the whole dominion, it is decided what is good and what evil, and where no

one does anything rightfully, save what he does in accordance with the general decree or consent (Sec. 16). For that, as we said in the last section, is wrong-doing, which cannot lawfully be committed, or is by law forbidden. But obedience is the constant will to execute that", which by law is good, and by the general decree ought to be done.

20. Yet we are accustomed to call that also wrong, which is done against the sentence of sound reason, and to give the name of obedience to the constant will to moderate the appetite according to the dictate of reason: a manner of speech which I should quite approve, did human liberty consist in the license of appetite, and slavery in the dominion of reason. But as human liberty is the greater, the more man can be guided by reason, and moderate his appetite, we cannot without great impropriety call a rational life obedience, and give the name of wrong-doing to that which is, in fact, a weakness of the mind, not a license of the mind directed against itself, and for which a man may be called a slave, rather than free (Secs. 7 and 11).

21. However, as reason teaches one to practice piety, and be of a calm and gentle spirit, which cannot be done save under dominion; and, further, as it is impossible for a multitude to be guided, as it were, by one mind, as under dominion is required, unless it has laws ordained according to the dictate of reason; men who are accustomed to live under dominion are not, therefore, using words so improperly, when they call that wrong-doing which is done against the sentence of reason, because the laws of the best dominion ought to be framed according to that dictate (Sec. 18). But, as for my saying (Sec. 18) that man in a state

of nature, if he does wrong at all, does it against himself, see, on this point, Chap. IV., Secs. 4, 5, where is shown, in what sense we can say, that he who holds dominion and possesses natural right, is bound by laws and can do wrong.

22. As far as religion is concerned, it is further clear, that a man is most free and most obedient to himself when he most loves God, and worships him in sincerity. But so far as we regard, not the course of nature, which we do not understand, but the dictates of reason only, which respect religion, and likewise reflect that these dictates are revealed to us by God, speaking, as it were, within ourselves, or else were revealed to prophets as laws; so far, speaking in human fashion, we say that man obeys God when he worships him in sincerity, and, on the contrary, does wrong when he is led by blind desire. But, at the same time, we should remember that we are subject to God's authority, as clay to that of the potter, who of the same lump makes some vessels unto honor, and others unto dishonor./7 And thus man can, indeed, act contrarily to the decrees of God, as far as they have been written like laws in the minds of ourselves or the prophets, but against that eternal decree of God, which is written in universal nature, and has regard to the course of nature as a whole, he can do nothing.

23. As, then, wrong—doing and obedience, in their strict sense, so also justice and injustice cannot be conceived of, except under dominion. For nature offers nothing that can be called this man's rather than another's; but under nature everything belongs to all ——that is, they have authority to claim it for themselves. But under dominion, where it is by common law determined what

belongs to this man, and what to that, he is called just who has a constant will to render to every man his own, but he unjust who strives, on the contrary, to make his own that which belongs to another.

24. But that praise and blame are emotions of joy and sadness, accompanied by an idea of human excellence or weakness as their cause, we have explained in our Ethics.

CHAPTER III.

OF THE RIGHT OF SUPREME AUTHORITIES.

UNDER every dominion the state is said to be Civil; but the entire body subject to a dominion is called a Commonwealth, and the general business of the dominion, subject to the direction of him that holds it, has the name of Affairs of State. Next we call men Citizens, as far as they enjoy by the civil law all the advantages of the commonwealth, and Subjects, as far as they are bound to obey its ordinances or laws. Lastly, we have already said that, of the civil state, there are three kinds—democracy, aristocracy, and monarchy (Chap. II. Sec. 17). Now, before I begin to treat of each kind separately, I will first deduce all the properties of the civil state in general. And of these, first of all comes to be considered the supreme right of the commonwealth, or the right of the supreme authorities.

2. From Chap. II. Sec. 15, it is clear that the right of the supreme authorities is nothing else than simple natural right, limited, indeed, by the power, not of every individual, but of the multitude, which is guided, as it were, by one mind—that is, as each individual in the state of nature, so the body and mind of a

dominion have as much right as they have power. And thus each single citizen or subject has the less right, the more the commonwealth exceeds him in power (Chap. II. Sec. 16), and each citizen consequently does and has nothing, but what he may by the general decree of the commonwealth defend.

3. If the commonwealth grant to any man the right, and therewith the authority (for else it is but a gift of words, Chap. II. Sec. 12), to live after his own mind, by that very act it abandons its own right, and transfers the same to him, to whom it has given such authority. But if it has given this authority to two or more, I mean authority to live each after his own mind, by that very act it has divided the dominion, and if, lastly, it has given this same authority to every citizen, it has thereby destroyed itself, and there remains no more a commonwealth, but everything returns to the state of nature; all of which is very manifest from what goes before. And thus it follows, that it can by no means be conceived, that every citizen should by the ordinance of the commonwealth live after his own mind, and accordingly this natural right of being one's own judge ceases in the civil state. I say expressly "by the ordinance of the commonwealth," for, if we weigh the matter aright, the natural right of every man does not cease in the civil state. For man, alike in the natural and in the civil state, acts according to the laws of his own nature, and consults his own interest. Man, I say, in each state is led by fear or hope to do or leave undone this or that; but the main difference between the two states is this, that in the civil state all fear the same things, and all have the same ground of security, and manner of life; and this certainly does not do away with the individual's faculty of

judgment. For he that is minded to obey all the commonwealth's orders, whether through fear of its power or through love of quiet, certainly consults after his own heart his own safety and interest.

4. Moreover, we cannot even conceive, that every citizen should be allowed to interpret the commonwealth's decrees or laws. For were every citizen allowed this, he would thereby be his own judge, because each would easily be able to give a color of right to his own deeds, which by the last section is absurd.

5. We see then, that every citizen depends not on himself, but on the commonwealth, all whose commands he is bound to execute, and has no right to decide, what is equitable or iniquitous, just or unjust. But, on the contrary, as the body of the dominion should, so to speak, be guided by one mind, and consequently the will of the commonwealth must be taken to be the will of all; what the state decides to be just and good must be held to be so decides by every individual. And so, however iniquitous the subject may think the commonwealth's decisions, he is none the less bound to execute them.

6. But (it may be objected) is it not contrary to the dictate of reason to subject one's self wholly to the judgment of another, and consequently, is not the civil state repugnant to reason? "Thence it would follow, that the civil state is irrational, and could only be created by men destitute of reason, not at all by such as are led by it. But since reason teaches nothing contrary to nature, sound reason cannot therefore dictate, that every one should remain independent, so long as men are liable to passions (Chap. II. Sec.

15), that is, reason pronounces against such independence (Chap. I. See. 5). Besides, reason altogether teaches to seek peace, and peace cannot be maintained, unless the commonwealth's general laws be kept unbroken. And so, the more a man is guided by reason, that is (Chap. II. Sec. 11), the more he is free, the more constantly he will keep the laws of the commonwealth, and execute the commands of the supreme authority, whose subject he is. Furthermore, the civil state is naturally ordained to remove general fear, and prevent general sufferings, and therefore pursues above everything the very end, after which every- one, Who is led by reason, strives, but in the natural state strives vainly (Chap. II. Sec. 15). Wherefore, if a man, who is led by reason, has sometimes to do by the commonwealth's order what he knows to be repugnant to reason, that harm is far compensated by the good, which he derives from the existence of a civil state. For it is reason's own law, to choose the less of two evils; and accordingly we may conclude, that no one is acting against the dictate of his own reason, so far as he does what by the law of the commonwealth is to be done. And this anyone will more easily grant us, after we have explained, how far the power and consequently the right of the commonwealth extends.

7. For first of all, it must be considered, that, as in the state of nature the man who is led by reason is most powerful and most independent, so too that commonwealth will be most powerful and most independent, which is founded and guided by reason. For the right of the commonwealth is determined by the power of the multitude, which is led, as it were, by one mind. But this

unity of mind can in no wise be conceived, unless the commonwealth pursues chiefly the very end, which sound reason teaches is to the interest of all men.

8. In the second place it comes to be considered, that subjects are so far dependent not on themselves, but on the commonwealth, as they fear its power or threats, or as they love the civil state (Chap. II. Sect. IO). Whence it follows, that such things, as no one can be induced to do by rewards or threats, do not fall within the rights of the commonwealth. For instance, by reason of his faculty of judgment, it is in no man's power to believe. For by what rewards or threats call a man be brought to believe, that the whole is not greater than its part, or that God does not exist, or that that is an infinite being, which he sees to be finite, or generally anything contrary to his sense or thought? So, too, by what rewards or threats can a man be brought to love one, whom he hates, or to hate one, whom he loves? And to this head must likewise be referred such things as are so abhorrent to human nature, that it regards them as actually worse than any evil, as that a man should be witness against himself, or torture himself, or kill his parents, or not strive to avoid death, and the like, to which no one can be induced by rewards or threats. But if we still choose to say, that the commonwealth has the right or authority to order such things, we can conceive of it in no other sense, than that in which one might say, that a man has the right to be mad or delirious. For what but a delirious fancy would such a right he, as could bind no one? And here I am speaking expressly of such things as cannot be subject to the right of a commonwealth and are abhorrent to human nature in general. For the fact, that a feel

or madman can by no rewards or threats be induced to execute orders, or that this or that person, because he is attached to this or that religion, judges the laws of a dominion worse than any possible evil, in no wise makes void the laws of the commonwealth, since by them most of the citizens are restrained. And so, as those who are without fear or hope are so far independent (Chap. II. Sec. 10), they are, therefore, enemies of the dominion (Chap. II. Sec. 14), and may lawfully be coerced by force.

9. Thirdly and lastly, it comes to be considered, that those things are not so much within the commonwealth's right, which cause indignation in the majority. For it is certain, that by the guidance of nature men conspire together, either through common fear, or with the desire to avenge some common hurt; and as the right of the commonwealth is determined by the common power of the multitude, it is certain that the power and right of the commonwealth are so far diminished, as it gives occasion for many to conspire together. There are certainly some subjects of fear for a commonwealth, and as every separate citizen or in the state of nature every man, so a commonwealth is the less independent, the greater reason it has to fear. So much for the right of supreme authorities over subjects. Now before I treat of the right of the said authorities as against others, we had better resolve a question commonly mooted about religion.

10. For it may be objected to us, Do not the civil state, and the obedience of subjects, such as we have shown is required in the civil state, do away with religion, whereby we are bound to worship God? But if we consider the matter, as it really is, we shall

find nothing that can suggest a scruple. For the mind, so far as it makes use of reason, is dependent, not on the supreme authorities, but on itself (Chap. II. Sec. 11). And so the true knowledge and the love of God cannot be subject to the dominion of any, nor yet can charity towards one's neighbor (Sec. 8). And if we further reflect, that the highest exercise of charity is that which aims at keeping peace and joining in unity, we shall not doubt that he does his duty, who helps everyone, so far as the commonwealth's laws, that is so far as unity and quiet allow. As for external rites, it is certain, that they can do no good or harm at all in respect of the true knowledge of God, and the love which necessarily results from it; and so they ought not to be held of such importance, that it should be thought worthwhile on their account to disturb public peace and quiet. Moreover it is "certain, that I am not a champion of religion by the law of nature, that is (Chap. II. Sec. 3), by the divine decree. For I have no authority, as once the disciples of Christ had, to cast out unclean spirits and work miracles; which authority is yet so necessary to the propagating of religion in places where it is forbidden, that without it one not only, as they say, wastes one's time/8 and trouble, but causes besides very many inconveniences, whereof all ages have seen most mournful examples. Everyone therefore, wherever he may be, can worship God with true religion, and mind his own business, which is the duty of a private man. But the care of propagating religion should be left to God, or the supreme authorities, upon whom alone falls the charge of affairs of state. But I return to my subject.

11. After explaining the right of supreme authorities over citizens

and the duty of subjects, it remains to consider the right of such authorities against the world at large, which is now easily intelligible from what has been said. For since (See. 2) the right of the supreme authorities is nothing else but simple natural right, it follows that two dominions stand towards each other in the same relation as do two men in the state of nature, with this exception, that a commonwealth can provide against being oppressed by another; which a man in the state of nature cannot do, seeing that he is overcome daily by sleep, often by disease or mental infirmity, and in the end by old age, and is besides liable to other inconveniences, from which a commonwealth can secure itself.

12. A commonwealth then is so far independent, as it can plan and provide against oppression by another (Chap. 11. Secs. 9, 15), and so far dependent on another commonwealth, as it fears that other's power, or is hindered by it from executing its own wishes, or lastly, as it needs its help for its own preservation or increase (Chap. II. Sees. 10, 15). For we cannot at all doubt, that if two commonwealths are willing to offer each other mutual help, both together are more powerful, and therefore have more right, than either alone (Chap. II. Sec. 13).

13. But this will be more clearly intelligible, if we reflect, that two commonwealths are naturally enemies. For men in the state of nature are enemies (Chap. 11. Sec. 14). Those, then, who stand outside a commonwealth, and retain their natural rights, continue enemies. Accordingly, if one commonwealth wishes to make war on another and employ extreme measures to make that other dependent on itself, it may lawfully make the attempt, since

it needs' but the bare will of the commonwealth for war to be waged. But concerning peace it can decide nothing, save with the concurrence of another commonwealth's will. Whence it follows, that laws of war regard every commonwealth by itself, but laws of peace regard not one, but at the least two commonwealths, which are therefore called "contracting powers."

14. This "contract" remains so long unmoved as the motive for entering into it, that is, fear of hurt or hope of gain, subsists. But take away from either commonwealth this hope or fear, and it is left independent (Chap. II. Sec. 10), and the link, whereby the commonwealths were mutually bound, breaks of itself. And therefore every commonwealth has the right to break its contract, whenever it chooses, and cannot be said to act treacherously or perfidiously in breaking its word, as soon as the motive of hope or fear is removed. For every contracting party was on equal terms in this respect, that whichever could first free itself of fear should be independent, and make use of its independence after its own mind; and, besides, no one makes a contract respecting the future, but on the hypothesis of certain precedent circumstances. But when these circumstances change, the reason of policy applicable to the whole position changes with them; and therefore every one of the contracting commonwealths retains the right of consulting its own interest, and consequently endeavors, as far as possible, to be free from fear and thereby independent, and to prevent another from coming out of the contract with greater power. If then a common-wealth complains that it has been deceived, it cannot properly blame the bad faith of another contracting commonwealth, but only its own folly in

having entrusted its own welfare to another party, that was independent, and had for its highest law the welfare of its own dominion.

15. To commonwealths, which have contracted a treaty of peace, it belongs to decide the questions, which may be mooted about the terms or rules of peace, whereby they have mutually bound themselves, inasmuch as laws of peace regard not one commonwealth, but the commonwealths which contract taken together (See. 13). But if they cannot agree together about the conditions, they by that very fact return to a state of war.

16. The more commonwealths there are, that have contracted a joint treaty of peace, the less each of them by itself is an object of fear to the remainder, or the less it has the authority to make war. But it is so much the more bound to observe the conditions of peace; that is (See. 13), the less independent, and the more bound to accommodate itself to the general will of the contracting parties.

17. But the good faith, inculcated by sound reason and religion, is not hereby made void; for neither reason nor Scripture teaches one to keep one's word in every case. For if I have promised a man, for instance, to keep safe a sum of money he has secretly deposited with me, I am not bound to keep my word, from the time that I know or believe the deposit to have been stolen, but I shall act more rightly in endeavoring to restore it to its owners. So likewise, if the supreme authority has promised another to do something, which subsequently occasion or reason shows or seems to show is contrary to the welfare of its subjects, it is surely

bound to break its word. As then Scripture only teaches us to keep our word in general, and leaves to every individual's judgment the special cases of exception, it teaches nothing repugnant to what we have just proved.

18. But that I may not have so often to break the thread of my discourse, and to resolve hereafter similar objections, I would have it known that all this demonstration of mine proceeds from the necessity of human nature, considered in what light you will —I mean, from the universal effort of all men after self-preservation, an effort inherent in all men, whether learned or unlearned. And therefore, however one considers men are led, whether by passion or by reason, it will he the same thing; for the demonstration, as we have said, is of universal application.

CHAPTER IV.

OF THE FUNCTIONS OF SUPREME AUTHORITIES.

That the right of the supreme authorities is limited by their power, we showed in the last chapter, and saw that the most important part of that right is, that they are, as it were, the mind of the dominion, whereby all ought to be guided; and accordingly, that such authorities alone have the right of deciding what is good, evil, equitable, or iniquitous, that is, what must be done or left undone by the subjects severally or collectively. And, accordingly, we saw that they have the sole right of laying down laws, and of interpreting the same, whenever their meaning is disputed, and of deciding whether a given case is in conformity with or violation of the law (Chap. III. Secs. 3-5); and, lastly, of waging war, and of drawing up and offering propositions for peace, or of accepting such when offered (Chap. III. Secs. 12, 13).

2. As all these functions, and also the means required to execute them, are matters which regard the whole body of the dominion, that is, are affairs of state, it follows, that affairs of state depend on the direction of him only, who holds supreme dominion. And hence it follows, that it is the right of the supreme authority alone to judge the deeds of every individual, and demand of him an account of the same; to punish criminals, and decide questions of law between citizens, or appoint jurists acquainted with the existing laws, to administer these matters on its behalf; and, further, to use and order all means to war and peace, as to found and fortify cities, levy soldiers, assign military posts, and order what it would have done, and, with a view to peace, to send and give audience to ambassadors; and, finally, to levy the costs of all this.

3. Since, then, it is the right of the supreme authority alone to handle public matters, or choose officials to do so, it follows, that that subject is a pretender to the dominion, who, without the supreme council's knowledge, enters upon any public matter, although he believe that his design will be to the best interest of the commonwealth.

4. But it is often asked, whether the supreme authority is bound by laws, and, consequently, whether it can do wrong. Now as the words "law" and "wrong-doing" often refer not merely to the laws of a commonwealth, but also to the general rules which concern all natural things, and especially to the general rules of reason, we

cannot, without qualification, say that the commonwealth is bound by no laws, or can do no wrong. For were the commonwealth bound by no laws or rules, which removed, the commonwealth were no commonwealth, we should have to regard it not as a natural thing, but as a chimera. A commonwealth then does wrong, when it does, or suffers to be done, things which may be the cause of its own ruin; and we can say that it then does wrong, in the sense in which philosophers or doctors say that nature does wrong; and in this sense we can say, that a commonwealth does wrong, when it acts against the dictate of reason. For a commonwealth is most independent when it acts according to the dictate of reason (Chap. III. Sec. 7); so far, then, as it acts against reason, it fails itself, or does wrong. And we shall be able more easily to understand this if we reflect, that when we sav, that a man can do what he will with his own, this authority must be limited not only by the power of the agent, but by the capacity of the object. If, for instance, I say that I can rightfully do what I will with this table, I do not certainly mean, that I have the right to make it eat grass. So, too, though we say, that men depend not on themselves, but on the commonwealth, we do not mean, that men lose their human nature. and put on another; nor yet that the commonwealth has the right to make men wish for this or that, or (what is just as impossible) regard with honor things which excite ridicule or disgust. But it is implied, that there are certain intervening circumstances, which supposed, one likewise supposes the reverence and fear of the subjects towards the commonwealth, and which abstracted, one makes abstraction likewise of that fear and reverence, and therewith of the commonwealth itself. The commonwealth, then, to maintain its independence, is bound to preserve the causes of fear and reverence, otherwise it ceases to be a commonwealth. For the person or persons that hold dominion, can no more combine with the keeping up of majesty the running with harlots drunk or naked about the streets, or the performances of a stage-player, or the open violation or contempt of laws passed by themselves, than they can combine existence with non-existence. But to proceed to slay and rob subjects, ravish maidens, and the like, turns fear into indignation and the civil state into a state of enmity.

5. We see, then, in what sense we may say, that a commonwealth is bound by laws and can do wrong. But if by "law" we understand civil law, and by " wrong" that which, by civil law, is forbidden to be done, that is, if these words be taken in their proper sense, we cannot at all say, that a commonwealth is bound by laws, or can do wrong. For the maxims and motives of fear and reverence, which a commonwealth is bound to observe in its own interest, pertain not to civil jurisprudence, but to the law of nature, since (Sec. 4:) they cannot be vindicated by the civil law, but by the law of war. And a commonwealth is bound by them in no other sense than that in which in the state of nature a man is bound to take heed, that he preserve his independence and be not his own enemy, lest he should destroy himself; and in this taking heed lies not the subjection, but the liberty of human nature. But civil jurisprudence depends on the mere decree of the commonwealth, which is not bound to please any but itself, nor to hold anything to be good or bad, but what it judges to be such for itself. And, accordingly, it has not merely the right to avenge

itself, or to lay down and interpret laws, but also to abolish the same, and to pardon any guilty person out of the fulness of its power.

6. Contracts or laws, whereby the multitude transfers its right to one council or man, should without doubt be broken, when it is expedient for the general welfare to do so. But to decide this point, whether, that is, it be expedient for the general welfare to break them or not. is within the right of no private person, but of him only who holds dominion (Sec. 3); therefore of these laws he who holds dominion remains sole interpreter. Moreover, no private person can by right vindicate these laws, and so they do not really bind him who holds dominion. Notwithstanding, if they are of such a nature that they cannot be broken, without at the same time weakening the Commonwealth's strength, that is, without at the same time changing to indignation the common fear of most of the citizens, by this very fact the commonwealth is dissolved, and the contract comes to an end ; and therefore such contract is vindicated not by the civil law, but by the law of war. And so he who holds dominion is not bound to observe the terms of the contract by any other cause than that, which bids a man in the state of nature to beware of being his own enemy, lest he should destroy himself, as we said in the last section.

CHAPTER V.

OF THE BEST STATE OF A DOMINION.

In Chap. II. Sec. 2, we showed, that man is then most independent, when he is most led by reason, and, in consequence

(Chap. III. Sec. 7), that that commonwealth is most powerful and most independent, which is founded and guided by reason. But, as the best plan of living, so as to assure to the utmost self-preservation, is that which is framed according to the dictate of reason, therefore it follows, that that in every kind is best done, which a man or commonwealth does, so far as he or it is in the highest degree independent. For it is one thing to till a field by right, and another to till it in the best way. One thing, I say, to defend or preserve one's self, and to pass judgment by right, and another to defend or preserve one's self in the best way, and to pass the best judgment; and, consequently, it is one thing to have dominion and care of affairs of state by right, and another to exercise dominion and direct afiairs of state in the best way. And so, as we have treated of the right of every commonwealth in general, it is time to treat of the best state of every dominion.

2. Now the quality of the state of any dominion is easily perceived from the end of the civil state, which end is nothing else but peace and security of life. And therefore that dominion is the best, where men pass their lives in unity, and the laws are kept unbroken. For it is certain, that seditions, wars, and contempt or breach of the laws are not so much to be imputed to the wickedness of the subjects, as to the bad state of a dominion. For men are not born fit for citizenship, but must be made so. Besides, men's natural passions are everywhere the same; and if wickedness more prevails, and more offenses are committed in one commonwealth than in another, it is certain that the former has not enough pursued the end of unity, nor framed its laws with sufficient forethought; and that, therefore, it has failed in making quite

good its right as a commonwealth. For a civil state, which 11as not done away with the causes of seditious, Where war is a perpetual object of fear, and where, lastly, the laws are often broken, differs but little from the mere state of nature, in which everyone lives after his own mind at the great risk of his life.

3. But as the vices and inordinate license and contumacy of subjects must be imputed to the commonwealth, so, on the other hand, their virtue and constant obedience to the laws are to be ascribed in the main to the virtue and perfect right of the commonwealth, as is clear from Chap. II. Sec. 15. And so it is deservedly reckoned to Hannibal as an extraordinary virtue, that in his army there never arose a. sedition./9

4. Of a commonwealth, whose subjects are but hindered by terror from taking arms, it should rather be said, that it is free from war, than that it has peace. For peace is not mere absence of war, but is a virtue that springs from force of character: for obedience (Chap. II. Sec. 19) is the constant will to execute what, by the general decree of the commonwealth, ought to be done. Besides that commonwealth, whose peace depends on the sluggishness of its subjects, that are led about like sheep, to learn but slavery, may more properly be called a desert than a commonwealth.

5. When, then, we call that dominion best, where men pass their lives in unity, I understand a human life, defined not by mere circulation of the blood, and other qualities common to all animals, but above all by reason, the true excellence and life of the mind.

6. But be it remarked that, by the dominion which I have said is

established for this end, I intend that which has been established by a free multitude, not that which is acquired over a multitude by right of war. For a free multitude is guided more by hope than fear; a conquered one, more by fear than hope: inasmuch as the former aims at making use of life, the latter but at escaping death. The former, I say, aims at living for its own ends, the latter is forced to belong to the conqueror; and so we say that this is enslaved, but that free. And, therefore, the end of a dominion, which one gets by right of war, is to be master, and have rather slaves than subjects. And although between the dominion created by a free multitude, and that gained by right of war, if We regard generally the right of each, we can make no essential distinction; yet their ends, as we have already shown, and further the means to the preservation of each are very different.

7. But what means a prince, whose sole motive is lust of mastery, should use to establish and maintain his dominion, the most ingenious Machiavelli has set forth at large,/10 but with what design one can hardly be sure. If, however, he had some good design, as one should believe of a learned man, it seems to have been to show, with how little foresight many attempt to remove a tyrant, though thereby the causes which make the prince a tyrant can in no wise be removed, but, on the contrary, are so much the more established, as the prince is given more cause to fear, which happens when the multitude has made an example of its prince, and glories in the parricide as in a thing well done. Moreover, he perhaps wished to show how cautious a free multitude should be of entrusting its welfare absolutely to one man, who, unless in his vanity he thinks he can please everybody, must be in daily fear of

plots, and so is forced to look chiefly after his own interest, and, as for the multitude, rather to plot against it than consult its good. And I am the more led to this opinion concerning that most farseeing man, because it is known that he was favorable to liberty, for the maintenance of which he has besides given the most wholesome advice.

CHAPTER VI.

OF MONARCHY.

Inasmuch as men are led, as we have said, more by passion than reason, it follows, that a multitude comes together, and wishes to be guided, as it were, by one mind, not at the suggestion of reason, but of some common passion——that is (Chap. III. Sec. 9), common hope, or fear, or the desire of avenging some common hurt. But since fear of solitude exists in all men, because no one in solitude is strong enough to defend himself, and procure the necessaries of life, it follows that men naturally aspire to the civil state; nor can it happen that men should ever utterly dissolve it.

.2. Accordingly, from the quarrels and seditious which are often stirred up in a commonwealth, it never results that the citizens dissolve it, as often happens in the case of other associations; but only that they change its form into some other——that is, of course, if the disputes cannot be settled, and the features of the commonwealth at the same time preserved. Wherefore, by means necessary to preserve a dominion, I intend such things as are necessary to preserve the existing form of the dominion, without any notable change.

3. But if human nature were so constituted, that men most desired

what is most useful, no art would be needed to produce unity and confidence. But, as it is admittedly far otherwise with human nature, a dominion most of necessarily be so ordered, that all, governing and governed alike, whether they will or no, shall do what makes for the general welfare; that is, that all, whether of their own impulse, or by force or necessity, shall be compelled to live according to the dictate of reason. And this is the case, if the affairs of the dominion be so managed, that nothing which affects the general welfare is entirely entrusted to the good faith of any one. For no man is so watchful, that he never falls asleep; and no man ever had a character so vigorous and honest, but he sometimes, and that just when strength of character was most wanted, was diverted from his purpose and let himself be overcome. And it is surely folly to require of another what one can never obtain from one's self; I mean, that he should be more watchful for another's interest than his own, that he should be free from avarice, envy, and ambition, and so on; especially when he is one, who is subject daily to the strongest temptations of every passion.

4:. But, on the other hand, experience is thought to teach, that it makes for peace and concord, to confer the whole authority upon one man. For no dominion has stood so long without any notable change, as that of the Turks, and on the other hand there were none so little lasting, as those, which were popular or democratic, nor any in which so many seditions arose. Yet if slavery, barbarism, and desolation are to be called peace, men can have no worse misfortune. No doubt there are usually more and sharper quarrels between parents and children, than between masters and slaves; yet it advances not the art of housekeeping, to change a father's right into a right of property, and count children but as slaves. Slavery then, not peace, is furthered by handing over to one man the whole authority. For peace, as we said before, consists not in mere absence of war, but in a union or agreement of minds,

5. And in fact they are much mistaken, who suppose that one man can by himself hold the supreme right of a commonwealth. For the only limit of right, as we showed (Chap. II.), is power. But the power of one man is very inadequate to support so great a load. And hence it arises, that the man, whom the multitude has chosen king, looks out for himself generals, or counsellors, or friends, to whom he entrusts his own and the common welfare; so that the dominion, which is thought to be a perfect monarchy, is in actual working an aristocracy, not, indeed, an open but a hidden one, and therefore the worst of all. Besides which, a king, who is a boy, or is, or overcome by age, is but king on sufferance; and those in this case have the supreme authority, who administer the highest business of the dominion, or are near the king's person; not to mention, that a lascivious king often manages everything at the caprice of this or that mistress or minion. "I had heard," says Orsines, "that women once reigned in Asia, but for a eunuch to reign is some- thing new." /11

6. It is also certain, that a commonwealth is always in greater danger from its citizens than from its enemies; for the good are few. Whence it follows, that he, upon whom the whole right of the dominion has been conferred. will always be more afraid of citizens than of enemies, and therefore will look to his own safety,

and not try to consult his subjects' interests, but to plot against them, especially against those who are renowned for learning, or have influence through wealth.

7. It must besides be added, that kings fear their sons also more than they love them, and so much the more as the latter are skilled in the arts of war and peace, and endeared to the subjects by their virtues. Whence it comes, that kings try so to educate their sons, that they may have no reason to fear them. Wherein ministers very readily obey the king, and will be at the utmost pains, that the successor may be an inexperienced king, whom they can hold tightly in hand.

8. From all which it follows, that the more absolutely the commonwealth's right is transferred to the king, the less independent he is, and the more unhappy is the condition of his subjects. And so, that a monarchical do- minion may be duly established, it is necessary to la.y solid foundations, to build it on; from which may result to the monarch safety, and to the multitude peace; and, therefore, to lay them in such a way, that the Il1() ll2ll'('ll may then be most independent, when he most consults tho: multitude's welfare. But I will first briefly state, what. these foundations of a monarchical dominion are, and after- wards prove them in order.

9. One or more cities must be founded and fortified, whose citizens, whether they live within the walls, or outside for purposes of agriculture, are all to enjoy the same right in the commonwealth; yet on this condition, that every city provide an ascertained number of citizens for its own and the general

defense. But a city, which cannot supply this, must be held in subjection on other terms.

10. The militia must be formed out of citizens alone, none being exempt, and of no others. And, therefore, all are to be bound to have arms, and no one to be admitted into the number of the citizens, till he has learnt his drill, and promised to practice it at stated times in the year. Next, the militia of each clan is to be divided into battalions and regiments, and no captain of a battalion chosen, that is not acquainted with military engineering. Moreover, though the commanders of battalions and regiments are to be chosen for life, yet the commander of the militia of a whole clan is to be chosen only in time of war, to hold command for a year at most, without power of being continued or afterwards re-appointed. And these last are to be selected out of the king's counsellors, of whom we shall speak in the fifteenth and following sections, or out of those who have filled the post of counsellor.

11. The townsmen and countrymen of every city, that is, the whole of the citizens, are to be divided into clans, distinguished by some name and badge, and all persons born of any of these clans are to be received into the number of citizens, and their names inscribed on the roll of their clan, as soon as they have reached the age, when they can carry arms and know their duty; with the exception of those, who are infamous from some crime, or dumb, or mad, or menials supporting life by some servile office.

12. The fields, and the whole soil, and, if it can be managed, the

houses should be public property, that is, the property of him, who holds the right of the commonwealth: and let him let them at a yearly rent to the citizens, Whether townsmen or countrymen, and with this exception let them all be free or exempt from every kind of taxation in time of peace. And of this rent a part is to be applied to the defenses of the state, a part to the king's private use. For it is necessary in time of peace to fortify cities against war, and also to have ready ships and other munitions of war.

13. After the selection of the king from one of the clans, none are to be held noble, but his descendants, who are therefore to be distinguished by royal insignia from their own and the other clans.

14. Those male nobles, who are the reigning king's collaterals, and stand to him in the third or fourth degree of consanguinity, must not marry, and any children they may have had, are to be accounted bastards, and unworthy of any dignity, nor may they be recognized as heirs to their parents, Whose goods must revert to the king.

15. Moreover the king's counsellors, who are next to him in dignity, must be numerous, and chosen out of the citizens only; that is (supposing there to be no more than six hundred clans) from every clan three or four or five, who will form together one section of this council; and not for life, but for three, four, or five years, so that every year a third, fourth, or fifth part may be replaced by selection, in which selection it must be observed as a first condition. that out of every clan at least one counsellor chosen be a jurist.

16. The selection must be made by the king himself, who should fix a time of year for the choice of fresh counsellors. Each clan must then submit to the king the names of all its citizens, who have reached their fiftieth year, and have been duly put forward as candidates for this office, and out of these the king will choose whom he pleases. But in that year, when the jurist of any clan is to be replaced, only the names of jurists are to be submitted to the king. Those who have filled this office of counsellor for the appointed time, are not to be continued therein, nor to be replaced on the list of candidates for five years or more. But the reason why one is to be chosen every year out of every clan is, that the council may not be composed alternately of untried novices, and of veterans versed in affairs, which must necessarily be the case, were all to retire at once, and new men to succeed them. But if every year one be chosen out of every family, then only a fifth, fourth, or at most a third part of the council will consist of novices. Further, if the king be prevented by other business, or for any other reason, from being able to spare time for this choice, then let the counsellors themselves choose others for a time, until the king either chooses different ones, or confirms the choice of the council.

17. Let the primary function of this council be to defend the fundamental laws of the dominion, and to give advice about administration, that the king may know, what for the public good ought to be decreed: and that on the understanding, that the king may not decide in any matter, without first hearing the opinion of this council. But if, as will generally happen, the council is not of one mind, but is divided in opinion, even after discussing the

same subject two or three times, there must be no further delay, but the different opinions are to be submitted to the king, as in the twenty fifth section of this chapter we shall show.

18. Let it be also the duty of this council to publish the king's orders or decrees, and to see to the execution of any decree concerning affairs of state, and to supervise the ad- ministration of the whole dominion, as the king's deputies.

19. The citizens should have no access to the king, save through this council, to which are to be handed all demands or petitions, that they may be presented to the king. Nor should the envoys of other commonwealths be allowed to obtain permission to address the king, but through the council. Letters, too, sent from elsewhere to the king, must be handed to him by the council. And in general the king is to be accounted as the mind of the commonwealth, but the council as the senses outside the mind, or the commonwealth's body, through whose intervention the mind understands the state of the commonwealth, and acts as it judges best for itself.

20. The care of the education of the king's sons should also fall on this council, and the guardianship, where a king has died, leaving as his successor an infant or boy. Yet lest meanwhile the council should be left without a king, one of the elder nobles of the commonwealth should be chosen to fill the king's place, till the legitimate heir has reached the age at which he can support the weight of government.

21. Let the candidates for election to this council be such as know the system of government, and the foundations, and state or

condition of the commonwealth, whose subjects they are. But he that would fill the place of a jurist must, besides the government and condition of the commonwealth, whose subject he is, be likewise acquainted with those of the other commonwealths, with which it has any intercourse. But none are to be placed upon the list of candidates, unless they have reached their fifth year without being convicted of crime.

22. In this council no decision is to be taken about the affairs of the dominion, but in the presence of all the members. But if anyone be unable through illness or other cause to attend, he must send in his stead one of the same clan, who has filled the oflice of counsellor or been put on the list of candidates. Which if he neglect to do, and the council through his absence be forced to adjourn any matter, let him be fined a considerable sum. But this must be understood to mean, when the question is of a matter affecting the whole dominion, as of peace or war, of abrogating or establishing a law, of trade, &c. But if the question be one that affects only a particular city or two, as about petitions, &c., it will suffice that a majority of the council attend.

23. To maintain a perfect equality between the clans, and a regular order in sitting, making proposals, and speaking, every clan is to take in turn the presidency at the sittings, a different clan at every sitting, and that which was first at one sitting is to be last at the next. But among members of the same clan, let precedence go by priority of election.

24. This council should be summoned at least four times a year, to demand of the ministers account of their administration of the

dominion, to ascertain the state of affairs, and see if anything else needs deciding. For it seems impossible for so large a number of citizens to have constant leisure for public business. But as in the meantime public business must none the less be carried on, therefore fifty or more are to be chosen out of this council to supply its place after its dismissal; and these should meet daily in a chamber next the kings and so have daily care of the treasury, the cities, the fortifications, the education of the king's son, and in general of all those duties of the great council, which we have just enumerated, except that they cannot take counsel about new matters, concerning which no decision has been taken.

25. On the meeting of the council, before anything is proposed in it, let five, six, or more jurists of the clans, which stand first in order of place at that session, attend on the king, to deliver to him petitions or letters, if they have any, to declare to him the state of affairs, and, lastly, to understand from him what he bids them propose in his council; and when they have heard this, let them return to the council, and let the first in precedence open the matter of debate. But, in matters which seem to any of them to be of some moment, let not the votes be taken at once, but let the voting be adjourned to such a date as the urgency of the matter allows. When, then, the council stands adjourned till the appointed time, the counsellors of every clan will meanwhile be able to debate the matter separately, and, if they think it of great moment, to consult others that have been counsellors, or are candidates for the council. And if within the appointed time the counsellors of any clan cannot agree among themselves, that clan shall lose its vote, for every clan can give but one vote. But,

otherwise, let the jurist of the clan lay before the council the opinion they have decided to be best; and so with the rest. And if the majority of the council think fit, after hearing the grounds of every opinion, to consider the matter again, let the council be again adjourned to a date, at which every clan shall pronounce its final opinion; and then, at last, before the entire council, let the votes be taken, and that opinion be invalidated which has not at least a hundred votes. But let the other opinions be submitted to the king by all the jurists present at the council, that, after hearing every party's arguments, he may select which opinion he pleases. And then let the jurists leave him, and return to the council; and there let all await the king at the time fixed by himself, that all may hear which opinion of those proposed he thinks fit to adopt, and what he decides should be done.

26. For the administration of justice, another council is to be formed of jurists, whose business should be to decide suits, and punish criminals, but so that all the judgments they deliver be tested by those who are for the time members of the great council ——that is, as to their having been delivered according to the due process of justice, and without partiality. But if the losing party can prove, that any judge has been bribed by the adversary, or that there is some mutual cause of friendship between the judge and the adversary, or of hatred between the judge and himself, or, lastly, that the usual process of justice has not been observed, let such party be restored to his original position. But this would, perhaps, not be observed by such as love to convict the accused in a criminal case, rather by torture than proofs. But, for all that. I can conceive on this point of no other process of justice than the

above, that befits the best system of governing a commonwealth.

27. Of these judges, there should be a large and odd number—for instance, sixty-one, or at least forty-one, and not more than one is to be chosen of one clan, and that not for life, but every year a certain proportion are to retire, and be replaced by as many others out of different clans, that have reached their fortieth year.

28. In this council, let no judgment be pronounced save in the presence of all the judges. But it any judges, from disease or other cause, shall for a long time be unable to attend the council. let another be chosen for that time to fill his place. But in giving their votes, they are all not to utter their opinions aloud, but to signify them by ballot.

29. Let those who supply others' places in this and the first-mentioned council first be paid out of the goods of those whom they have condemned to death, and also out of the lines of which any are muleted. Next, after every judgment they pronounce in a civil suit, let them receive a certain proportion of the whole sum at stake for the benefit of both councils.

30. Let there be in every city other subordinate councils, whose members likewise must not be chosen for life, but must. be partially renewed every year, out of the clans who live there only. But there is no need to pursue this further.

31. No military pay is to be granted in time of peace; but. in time of war, military pay is to be allowed to those only, who support their lives by daily labour. But the commanders and other officers of the battalions are to expect no other advantage from war but the spoil of the enemy.

32. If a foreigner takes to wife the daughter of a citizen, his children are to he counted citizens, and put on the roll of their mother's clan. But those who are born and bred within the dominion of foreign parents should be allowed to purchase at a fixed price the right of citizenship from the captains of thousands of any clan, and to be enrolled in that clan. For no harm can arise thence to the dominion, even though the captains of thousands, for a bribe, admit a foreigner into the number of their citizens for less than the fixed price; but, on the contrary, means should be devised for more easily increasing the number of citizens, and producing a large confluence of men. As for those who are not enrolled as citizens, it is but fair that, at least in war-time, they should pay for their exemption from service by some forced labour or tax.

33. The envoys to be sent in time of peace to other commonwealths must be chosen out of the nobles only, and their expenses met by the state treasury, and not the king's privy purse.

34. Those that attend the court, and are the king's servants, and are paid out of his privy purse, must be excluded from every appointment and office in the commonwealth. I say expressly, "and are paid out of the king's privy purse," to except the body-guard. For there should be no other body-guard, but the citizens of the king's city, who should take turns to keep guard at court before the king's door.

35. War is only to be made for the sake of peace, so that, at its end, one may be rid of arms. And so, when cities have been taken by right of war, and terms of peace are to be made after the enemies

are subdued, the captured cities must not be garrisoned and kept; but either the enemy, on accepting the terms of peace, should be allowed to redeem them at a price, or, if by following that policy, there would, by reason of the danger of the position, remain a constant lurking anxiety, they must be utterly destroyed, and the inhabitants removed elsewhere.

36. The king' must not be allowed to contract a foreign marriage, but only to take to wife one of his kindred, or of the citizens; yet. on condition that, if he marries a citizen, her near relations become incapable of holding office in the commonwealth.

37. The dominion must be indivisible. And so, if the king leaves more than one child, let the eldest one succeed; but by no means be it allowed to divide the dominion between them, or to give it undivided to all or several of them, much less to give a part of it as a daughter's dowry. For that daughters should be admitted to the inheritance of a dominion is in no wise to be allowed.

38. If the king die leaving: no male issue. let the next to him in blood be held the heir to the dominion, unless he chance to have married a foreign wife, whom he will not put away.

39. As for the citizens, it is manifest (Chap. Ill. See. 5) that every one of them ought to obey all the commands of the king, and the decrees published by the great council, although he believe them to be most absurd, and otherwise he may rightfully be forced to obey. And these are the foundations of a monarchical dominion, on which it must be built, it it is to be stable, as we shall show in the next chapter.

40. As for religion, no temples whatever ought to be built at the

public expense; nor ought laws to be established about opinions, unless they be seditious and overthrow the foundations of the commonwealth. And so let such as are allowed the public exercise of their religion build a temple at their own expense. But the king may have in his palace a chapel of his own, that he may practice the religion to which he belongs.

CHAPTER VII

OF MONARCHY (CONTINUATION).

After explaining the foundations of a monarchical dominion, I have taken in hand to prove here in order the fitness of such foundations. And to this end the first point to be noted is, that it is in no way repugnant to experience, for laws to be so firmly fixed, that not the king himself can abolish them. For though the Persians worshipped their kings as gods, yet had not the kings themselves authority to revoke laws once established, as appears from Daniel,/12 and nowhere, as far as I know, is a monarch chosen absolutely without any conditions expressed. Nor yet is it repugnant to reason or the absolute obedience due to a king. For the foundations of the dominion are to be considered as eternal decrees of the king, so that his ministers entirely obey him in refusing to execute his orders, when he commands anything contrary to the same. Which we can make plain by the example of Ulysses./13 For his comrades were executing his own order, when they would not untie him, when he was bound to the mast and captivated by the Sirens' song, although he gave them manifold orders to do so, and that with threats. And it is ascribed to his forethought, that he afterwards thanked his comrades for obeying him according to his first intention. And, after this example of Ulysses, kings often instruct judges, to administer justice without respect of persons, not even of the king himself, if by some singular accident he order anything contrary to established law. For kings are not gods, but men, who are often led captive by the Sirens' song. If then everything depended on the inconstant will of one man, nothing would be fixed. And so, that a monarchical dominion may be stable, it must be ordered, so that everything be done by the king's decree only, that is, so that every law be an explicit will of the king, but not every will of the king a law; as to which see Chap. VI. Sects. 3, 5, 6.

2. It must next be observed, that in laying foundations it is very necessary to study the human passions: and it is not enough to have shown, what ought to be done, but it ought, above all, to be shown how it can be affected, that men, whether led by passion or reason, should yet keep the laws firm and unbroken. For if the constitution of the dominion, or the public liberty depends only on the weak assistance of the laws, not only will the citizens have no security for its maintenance (as we showed in the third section of the last chapter), but it will even turn to their ruin. For this is certain, that no condition of a commonwealth is more wretched than that of the best, when it begins to totter, unless at one blow it falls with a rush into slavery, which seems to be quite impossible. And, therefore, it would be far better for the subjects to transfer their rights absolutely to one man, than to bargain for un-ascertained and empty, that is unmeaning , terms of liberty, and so prepare for their posterity a way to the most cruel servitude. But if I succeed in showing that the foundation of

monarchical dominion, which I stated in the last chapter, are firm and cannot be plucked up, without the indignation of the larger part of an armed multitude, and that from them follow peace and security for king and multitude, and if I deduce this from the general human nature, no one will be able to doubt, that these foundations are the best and the true ones (Chap. III. Sec. 9, and Chap. VI. Sects. 3, 8). But that such is their nature, I will show as briefly as possible.

3. That the duty of him, who holds the dominion, is always to know its state and condition, to watch over the common welfare of all, and to execute whatever is to the interest of the majority of the subjects, is admitted by all. But as one person alone is unable to examine into everything, and cannot always have his mind ready and turn it to meditation, and is often hindered by disease, or old age, or other causes, from having leisure for public business; therefore it is necessary that the monarch have counsellors to know the state of affairs, and help the king with their advice, and frequently supply his place; and that so it come to pass, that the dominion or commonwealth may continue always in one and the same mind.

4. But as human nature is so constituted, that everyone seeks with the utmost passion his own advantage, and judges those laws to be most equitable, which he thinks necessary to preserve and increase his substance, and defends another's cause so far only as he thinks he is thereby establishing his own; it follows hence, that the counsellors chosen must be such, that their private affairs and their own interests depend on the general welfare and peace of all. And so it is evident, that if from every sort or class of citizens

a certain number be chosen, what has most votes in such a council will be to the interest of the greater part of the subjects. And though this council, because it is composed of so large a number of citizens, must of necessity be attended by many of very simple intellect, yet this is certain, that everyone is pretty clever and sagacious in business which he has long and eagerly practiced. And, therefore, if none be chosen but such as have till their fiftieth year practiced their own business without disgrace, they will be fit enough to give their advice about their own affairs, especially if, in matters of considerable importance, a time be allowed for consideration. Besides, it is far from being the fact, that a council composed of a few is not frequented by this kind of men. For, on the contrary, its greatest part must consist of such, since everyone, in that case, tries hard to have dullards for colleagues, that they may hang on his words, for which there is no opportunity in large councils.

5. Furthermore, it is certain, that everyone would rather rule than be ruled. "For no one of his own will yields up dominion to another," as Sallust has it in his first speech to Caesar./14 And, therefore, it is clear, that a whole multitude will never transfer its right to a few or to one, if it can come to an agreement with itself, without proceeding from the controversies, which generally arise in large councils, to seditions. And so the multitude does not, if it is free, transfer to the king anything but that, which it cannot itself have absolutely within its authority, namely, the ending of controversies and the using despatch in decisions. For as to the case which often arises, where a king is chosen on account of war, that is, because war is much more happily conducted by kings, it

is manifest. folly, I say, that men should choose slavery in time of peace for the sake of better fortune in war; if, indeed, peace can be conceived of in a dominion, where merely for the sake of war the highest authority is transferred to one man, who is, therefore, best able to show his worth and the importance to everyone of his single self in time of war; whereas, on the contrary, democracy has this advantage, that its excellence is greater in peace than in war. However. for whatever reason a king is chosen, he cannot by himself, as we said just now, know what will be to the interest of the dominion: but for this purpose, as we showed in the last section, will need many citizens for his counsellors. And as we cannot at all suppose, that any opinion can be conceived about a matter proposed for discussion, which can have escaped the notice of so large a number of men, it follows, that no opinion can be conceived tending to the people's welfare, besides all the opinions of this council, which are submitted to the king. And so, since the people's welfare is the highest law, or the king's utmost right, it follows, that the king's utmost right is but to choose one of the opinions offered by the council, not to decree anything, or offer any opinion contrary to the mind of all the council at once (Chap. VI. Sec. 25). But if all the opinions offered in the council were to be submitted to the king, then it might happen that the king would always favor the small cities, which have the fewest votes. For though by the constitution of the council it be ordained, that the opinions should be submitted to the king without mention of their supporters, yet they will never be able to take such good care, but that some opinion will get divulged. And, therefore, it must of necessity be provided. that that opinion, which has not gained at least a hundred votes, shall be held void; and this law the larger cities will be sure to defend with all their might.

6. And here, did I not study brevity, I would show other advantages of this council; yet one, which seems of the greatest importance, I will allege. I mean, that there can be given no greater inducement to virtue, than this general hope of the highest honor. For by ambition are we all most led, as in our Ethics we showed to be the case/15

7. But it cannot be doubted that the majority of this council will never be minded to wage war, but rather always pursue and love peace. For besides that war will always cause them fear of losing their property and liberty, it is to be added, that war requires fresh expenditure, which they must meet, and also that their own children and relatives, though intent on their domestic cares, will be forced to turn their attention to war and go a-soldiering, whence they will never bring back anything but unpaid for scars. For, as we said (Chap. VI. Sec. 81), no pay is to be given to the militia, and (Chap. VI. Sec. 10) it is to be formed out of citizens only and no others.

8. There is another accession to the cause of peace and concord, which is also of great weight: I mean, that no citizen can have immovable property (Chap. VI. Sec. 12). Hence all will have nearly an equal risk in war. For all will be obliged, for the sake of gain, to practice trade, or lend money to one another, if, as formerly by the Athenians, a law be passed, forbidding to lend money at interest to any but inhabitants; and thus they will be

engaged in business, which either is mutually involved, one man's with another's, or needs the same means for its furtherance. And thus the greatest part of this council will generally have one and the same mind about their common affairs and the arts of peace. For, as we said (See. 4), every man defends another's cause, so far as he thinks thereby to establish his own.

9. It cannot be doubted, that it will never occur to anyone to corrupt this council with bribes. For were any man to draw over to his side some one or two out of so great a number of men, he would gain nothing. For, as we said, the opinion, which does not gain at least a hundred votes, is void.

10. We shall also easily see, that, once this council is established its members cannot be reduced to a. less number, if we consider the common passions of mankind. For all are guided mostly by ambition, and there is no man who lives in health but hopes to attain extreme old age. If then we calculate the number of those who actually reach their fiftieth or sixtieth year, and further take into account the number that are every year chosen of this great countil we shall see, that there can hardly he a man of those who hear arms, but is under the influence of a great hope of attaining this dignity. And so they will all, to the best of their power, defend this law of the council. For he it noted, that corruption, unless it creep in gradually, is easily prevented. But as it can be more easily supposed, and would he less invidious, that a less number should be chosen out of every clan, than that a less number should he chosen out of a few clans, or that one or two clans should he altogether excluded; therefore (Chap. VI. Sec. 15) the number of counsellors cannot be reduced, unless a third, fourth, or fifth part

he removed simultaneously, which change is a very great one, and therefore quite repugnant to common practice. Nor need one he afraid of delay or negligence in choosing, because this is remedied by the council itself. See Chap. VI. See. 16.

11. The king, then, whether he is induced by fear of the multitude, or aims at binding; to himself the majority of an armed multitude, or is guided by a generous spirit, a wish that is, to consult the public interest, will always confirm that opinion, which has gained most votes, that is (See. 5),/16 which is to the interest of the greater part of the dominion; and will study to reconcile the divergent opinions referred to him, if it can he done, that he may attach all to himself (in which he will exert all his powers), and that alike in peace and war they may find out, what an advantage his single self is to them. And thus he will then he most. independent, and most in possession of dominion, when he most consults the general welfare of the multitude.

12. For the king by himself cannot restrain all by fear. But his power, as we have said, rests upon the number of his soldiers, and especially on their valor and faith, which will always remain so long enduring between men, as with them is joined need, be that need honorable or disgraceful. And this is why kings usually are fender of exciting than restraining their soldiery, and shut their eyes more to their vices than to their virtues, and generally, to hold under the best of them, seek out, distinguish, and assist with money or favor the idle, and those who have mined themselves by debauchery, and shake hands with them, and throw them kisses, and for the sake of mastery stoop to every servile action. In order therefore that the citizens may be distinguished by the king before

all others, and, as far as the civil state and equity permit, may remain independent, it is necessary that the militia should consist of citizens only, and that citizens should be his counsellors; and on the contrary citizens are altogether subdued, and are laying the foundations of eternal war, from the moment that they suffer mercenaries to be levied, whose trade is war, and who have most power in strifes and seditions.

13. That the king's counsellors ought not to be elected for life, but for three, four, or five years, is clear as well from the tenth, as from what we said in the ninth section of this chapter. For if they were chosen for life, not only could the greatest part of the citizens conceive hardly any hope of obtaining this honor, and thus there would arise a great inequality, and thence envy, and constant murmurs, and at last seditious, which, no doubt, would be welcome to kings greedy of mastery: but also the counsellors, being rid of the fear of their successors, would assume a great license in all respects, which the king would be far from opposing. For the more the citizens hate them, the more they will cling to the king, and be ready to flatter him. Nay, the interval of five years seems even too much, for in such a space of time it does not seem so impossible to corrupt by bribes or favor a very large part of the council, however large it be. And therefore it will be far safer, if every year two out of every clan retire, and be replaced by as many more (supposing that there are to be five counsellors of each clan), except in the year in which the jurist of any clan retires, and a fresh one is chosen in his place.

14. Moreover, no king can promise himself more safety, than he who reigns in a commonwealth of this sort. For besides that a king

soon perishes, when his soldiers cease to desire his safety, it is certain that kings are always in the greatest danger from those who are nearest their persons. The fewer counsellors, then, there are, and the more powerful they consequently are, the more the king is in danger of their transferring the dominion to another. Nothing in fact more alarmed David, than that his own counsellor Ahitophel sided with Absalom./16 Still more is this the ease, if the whole authority has been transferred absolutely to one man, because it can then he more easily transferred from one to another. For two private soldiers once took in hand to transfer the Roman empire, and did transfer it./17 I omit the arts and cunning wiles, whereby counsellors have to assure themselves against falling victims to their un-popularity; for they are but too well known, and no one, who has read history, can he ignorant, that the good faith of counsellors has generally turned to their ruin. And so, for their own safety, it beloved them to he cunning, not faithful. But if the counsellors are too numerous to unite in the same crime, and are all equal, and do not hold their office beyond a period of four years, they cannot be at all objects of fear to the king, except he attempt to take away their liberty, wherein he will offend all the citizens equally. For, as Antonio Perez/18 excellently observes, an absolute dominion is to the prince very dangerous, to the subjects very hateful, and to the institutes of God and man alike opposed, as innumerable instances show.

15. Besides these we. have, in the last chapter, laid other foundations, lay which the king is greatly secured in his dominion. and the citizens in their hold of peace and liberty, which formulations we will reason out in their proper places. Fur

I was anxious above everything to reason out all those, which refer to the great council and are of the greatest importance Now l will continue with the others, in the same order in which I stated them.

16. It is undoubted, that citizens are more powerful, and, therefore, more independent, the larger and better fortified their towns are. For the safer the place is, in which they are, the better they can defend their liberty, and the less they need fear an enemy, whether without or within; and it is certain that the more powerful men are by their riches, the more they by nature study their own safety. But cities which need the help of another for their preservation are not on terms of equal right with that other, but are so far dependent on his right as they need his help. For we showed in the second chapter, that right is determined by power alone.

17. For the same reason, also, I mean that the citizens may continue independent, and defend their liberty, the militia ought to be composed of the citizens only, and none of them to be exempted. For an armed man is more independent than an unarmed (Sec. 12); and those citizens transfer absolutely their own right to another, and entrust it entirely to his good faith, who have given him their arms and the defenses of their cities. Human avarice, by which most men are very much led, adds its weight to this view. For it cannot be, that a mercenary force be hired without great expense; and citizens can hardly endure the exactions required to maintain an idle soldiery. But that no man, who commands the whole or a large part of the militia, should, except under pressure of necessity, be chosen for the extreme term of a

year, all are aware, who have read history, alike sacred and profane. For there is nothing that reason more clearly teaches. For surely the might of dominion is altogether entrusted to him, who is allowed enough time to gain military glory, and raise his fame above the king's, or to make the army faithful to himself by flattery, largesses, and the other arts, whereby generals are accustomed to procure the enslavement of others, and the mastery for themselves. Lastly, I have added this point for the greater safety of the whole dominion, that these commanders of the militia are to be selected from the king's counsellors or ex-counsellors——— that is, from men who have reached the age at which mankind generally prefer what is old and safe to what is new and dangerous./20

18. I said that the citizens were to he divided into clans,/21 and an equal number of counsellors chosen from each, in order that the larger towns might have, in proportion to the number of their citizens, a greater number of counsellors, and be able, as is equitable, to contribute more votes. For the power and, therefore, the right of a dominion is to be estimated by the number of its citizens; and I do not believe that any fitter means can be devised for maintaining this equality between citizens, who are all by nature so constituted, that everyone wishes to be attributed to his own stock, and be distinguished by race from the rest.

19. Furthermore, in the state of nature, there is nothing which any man can less claim for himself, and make his own, than the soil, and whatever so adheres to the soil, that he cannot hide it anywhere, nor carry it whither he pleases. The soil, therefore, and

whatever adheres to it in the way we have mentioned. must be quite common property of the commonwealth— that is, of all those who, by their united force, can vindicate their claim to it, or of him to whom all have given authority to vindicate his claim. And therefore the soil, and all that adheres to it, ought to have a value with the citizens proportionate to the necessity there is, that they may be able to set their feet thereon, and defend their common right or liberty. But in the eighth section of this chapter we have shown the advantages that the commonwealth must necessarily derive hence.

20. In order that the citizens may be as far as possible equal, which is of the first necessity in a commonwealth, none but the descendants of a king are to be though noble. But if all the descendants of kings were allowed to marry wives, or beget children, they would grow, in process of time, to a very large number, and would be, not only burdensome, but also a cause of very great fear, to king and all. For men who have too much leisure generally meditate crime. And hence it is that kings are, on account of their nobles, very much induced to make war, because kings surrounded with nobles find more quiet and safety in war than in peace. But I pass by this as notorious enough, and also the points which I have mentioned in Secs. 15-27 of the last chapter. For the main points have been proved in this chapter, and the rest are self-evident.

21. -That the judges ought to be too numerous for a large proportion of them to be accessible to the bribes of a private man, and that they should not vote openly, but secretly, and that they deserve payment for their time, is known to everyone./22 But they

everywhere have by custom a yearly salary; and so they make no great haste to determine suits, and there is often no end to trials. Next, where confiscations accrue to the king, there frequently in trials not truth nor right, but the greatness of a man's riches is regarded. Informers are ever at work, and everyone who has money is snatched as a prey, which evils, though grievous and intolerable, are excused by the necessity of warfare, and continue even in time of peace. But the avarice of judges that are appointed but for two or three years at most is moderated by fear of their successors, not to mention, again, that they can have no fixed property, but must lend their money at interest to their fellow-citizens. And so they are forced rather to consult their welfare than to plot against them, especially if the judges themselves, as we have said, are numerous.

22. But we have said, that no military pay is to be voted./23 For the chief reward of military service is liberty. For in the state of nature everyone strives, for bare liberty's sake, to defend himself to the utmost of his power, and expects no other reward of warlike virtue but his own independence. But, in the civil state, all the citizens together are to be considered as a man in the state of nature ; and, therefore, when all fight on behalf of that state, all are defending themselves, and engaged on their own business. But counsellors, judges, magistrates, and the like, are engaged more on others' business than on their own; and so it is but fair to pay them for their time. Besides, in war, there can be no greater or more honorable inducement to victory than the idea of liberty. But if, on the contrary, a certain portion of the citizens be designated as soldiers, on which account it will be necessary to

award them a fixed pay, the king will, of necessity, distinguish them above the rest (as we showed, See. 12) that is, will distinguish men who are acquainted only with the arts of war, and, in time of peace, from excess of leisure, become debauched, and finally, from poverty meditate nothing but rapine, civil discord, and wars. And so we can affirm, that a monarchy of this sort is, in fact, a state of war, and in it only the soldier enjoy liberty, but the rest are slaves.

23. Our remarks about the admission of foreigners (Chap. VI. Sec. 32) I believe to be obvious. Besides, no one can doubt that the king's blood-relations should be at a distance from him, and occupied, not by warlike, but by peaceful business, whence they may get credit and the dominion quiet. Though even this has not seemed a sufficient precaution to the 'Turkish despots, who, therefore, make a point of slaughtering all their brothers. And no wonder: for the more absolutely the right of dominion has been conferred on one man, the more easily, as we showed by an instance (Sec. 14), it can be transferred from one to another. But that in such a monarchy, as we here suppose, in which, I mean. there is not one mercenary soldier, the plan we have mentioned provides sufficiently for the king's safety, is not to be doubted.

24. Nor can anyone hesitate about what we have said in the, thirty-fourth and thirty-fifth sections of the last chapter. But that the king must not marry a foreigner/24 is easily proved. For not to mention that two commonwealths, although united by a. treaty, are yet in a state of hostility (Chap. Ill. See. 1-it), it is very much to be avoided that war should be stirred up, on account of the king's domestic affairs. Both because disputes and dissensions arise peculiarly

from an alliance founded on marriage, and because questions between two commonwealths are mostly settled by war. Of this we read a fatal instance in Scripture. For after the death of Solomon, who had married the king of Egypt's daughter, his son Rehoboam waged a most disastrous war with Shishak, king of the Egyptians, who utterly subdued him./25 Moreover, the marriage of Lewis XIV., king of France with the daughter of Philip IV was the seed of a fresh war./26 And, besides these, very many instances may be read in history.

25. The form of the dominion ought to be kept one and the same, and, consequently, there should be but one king, and that of the same sex, and the dominion should be indivisible./27 But as to my saying that the king's eldest son should succeed his father by right, or (if there be no issue) the nearest to him in blood, it is clear as well from Chap. VI. Sec. 13, as because the election of the king made by the multitude should, if possible, last for ever. Otherwise it will necessarily happen, that the supreme authority of the dominion will frequently pass to the multitude, which is an extreme and, therefore, exceedingly dangerous change. But those who, from the fact that the king is master of the dominion, and holds it by absolute right, infer that he can hand it over to whom he pleases, and that, therefore, the king's son is by right heir to the dominion, are greatly mistaken. For the king's will has so long the force of law, as he holds the sword of the commonwealth; for the right of dominion is limited by power only. Therefore, a king may indeed abdicate, but cannot hand the dominion over to another, unless with the concurrence of the multitude or its stronger part. And that this may be more clearly

understood, we must remark, that children are heirs to their parents, not by natural, but by civil law. For by the power of the commonwealth alone is anyone master of definite property. And, therefore, by the same power or right, whereby the will of any man concerning his property is held good, by the same also his will remains good after his own death, as long as the commonwealth endures. And this is the reason, why everyone in the civil state maintains after death the same right as he had in his lifetime, because, as we said, it is not by his own power, but by that of the commonwealth, which is everlasting, that he can decide anything about his property. But the king's case is quite different. For the king's will is the civil law itself, and the king the commonwealth itself. Therefore, by the death of the king, the commonwealth is in a manner dead, and the civil state naturally returns to the state of nature, and consequently the supreme authority to the multitude, which can, therefore, lawfully lay down new and abolish old laws. And so it appears that no man succeeds the king by right, but him whom the multitude wills to be successor, or in a theocracy, such as the common. wealth of the Hebrews once was, him whom God has chosen by a prophet. We might likewise infer this from the fact that the king's sword, or right, is is reality the will of the multitude itself, or its stronger part; or else from the fact, that men endowed with reason never so utterly abdicate their right, that they cease to be men, and are accounted as sheep. But to pursue this further is unnecessary.

26. But the right of religion, or of worshipping God, no man can transfer to another. However, we have treated of this point at length in the last chapters of our Theologico-Politieal Treatise,

which it is superfluous to repeat here. And herewith I claim to have reasoned out the foundations of the best monarchy, though briefly, yet with sufficient clearness. But their mutual interdependence, or, in other words, the proportions of my dominion. anyone will easily remark, who will be at the pains to observe them as a whole with some attention. It remains only to warn the reader, that I am here conceiving of that monarchy, which is instituted by a free multitude, for which alone these foundations can serve. For a multitude that has grown used to another form of dominion will not be able without great danger of overthrow to pluck up the accepted foundations of the whole dominion, and change its entire fabric.

27. And what we have written will, perhaps, be received with derision by those who limit to the populace only the vices which are inherent in all mortals; and use such phrases as, "the mob, if it is not frightened, inspires no little fear," and "the populace is either a humble slave, or a haughty master," and "it has no truth or judgment," etc. But all have one common nature. Only we are deceived by power and refinement. Whence it comes that when two do the same thing we say, " this man may do it with impunity, that man may not; " not because the deed, but because the doer is different. Haughtiness is a property of rulers. Men are haughty, but by reason of an appointment for a year; how much more then nobles, that have their honors eternal ! But their arrogance is glossed over with importance, luxury, profusion, and a kind of harmony of vices, and a certain cultivated folly, and elegant villainy, so that vices, each of which looked at separately is foul and vile, because it is then most conspicuous, appear to the

inexperienced and untaught honorable and becoming. "The mob, too, if it is not frightened, inspires no little fear; " yes, for liberty and slavery are not easily mingled. Lastly, as for the populace being devoid of truth and judgment, that is nothing wonderful, since the chief business of the dominion is transacted behind its back, and it can but make conjectures from the little, which cannot be hidden. For it is an uncommon virtue to suspend one's judgment. So it is supreme folly to wish to transact everything behind the backs of the citizens, and to expect that they will not judge ill of the same, and will not give everything an unfavorable interpretation. For if the populace could moderate itself, and suspend its judgment about things with which it is imperfectly acquainted, or judge rightly of things by the little it knows already, it would surely be more fit to govern, than to be governed. But, as we said, all have the same nature. All grow haughty with rule, and cause fear if they do not feel it, and everywhere truth is generally transgressed by enemies or guilty people; especially where one or a few have mastery, and have respect in trials not to justice or truth, but to amount of wealth.

28. Besides, paid soldiers, that are accustomed to military discipline, and can support cold and hunger, are likely to despise a crowd of citizens as very inferior for storming towns or fighting pitched battles. But that my dominion is, therefore, more unhappy or less durable, no one of sound mind will affirm. But, on the contrary, everyone that judges things fairly will admit, that that dominion is the most durable of all, which can content itself with preserving what it has got, without coveting what belongs to others, and strives, therefore, most eagerly by every means to

avoid war and preserve peace.

29. But I admit that the counsels of such a dominion can hardly be concealed. But everyone will also admit with me that it is far better for the right counsels of a dominion to be known to its enemies, than for the evil secrets of tyrants to be concealed from the citizens. They who can treat secretly of the affairs of a dominion have it absolutely under their authority, and, as they plot against the enemy in time of war, so do they against the citizens in time of peace. Now that this secrecy is often serviceable to a dominion, no one call deny; but that without it the said dominion cannot subsist, no one will ever prove. But, on the contrary, to entrust affairs of state absolutely to any man is quite incompatible with the maintenance of liberty; and so it is folly to choose to avoid a small loss by means of the greatest of evils. But the perpetual refrain of those who lust after absolute dominion is, that it is to the essential interest of the commonwealth that its business be secretly transacted, and other like pretenses, which end in the more hateful a slavery, the more they are clothed with a show of utility.

30. Lastly, although no dominion, as far as I know, has ever been founded on all the conditions we have mentioned, yet from experience itself we shall be able to prove that this form of monarchy is the best, if we consider the causes of the preservation and overthrow of any dominion that is not barbarous. But this I could not do without greatly wearying the reader. However, I cannot pass over in silence one instance, that seems worth remembering: I mean the dominion of the Arragonese, who showed a singular loyalty towards their kings, and with equal

constancy preserved unbroken the constitution of the kingdom. For as soon as they had cast off the slavish yoke of the Moors, they resolved to choose themselves a. king but on what conditions they could not quite make up their minds, and they therefore determined to consult the sovereign pontiff of Rome. He, who in this matter certainly bore himself as Christ.'s vicar, blamed them for so obstinately wishing to choose a king, unwarned by the example of the Hebrews. However. if they would not change their minds, then he advised them not to choose a king, without first instituting customs equitable and suitable to the national genius, and above all he would have them create some supreme council, to balance the king's power like the ephors of the Lacedaemonians, and to have absolute right to determine the disputes, which might arise between the king and the citizens. So then, following this advice, they established the laws, which seemed to them most equitable, of which the supreme interpreter, and therefore supreme judge, was to be, not the king, but the council, which they call the Seventeen, and whose president has the title of Justice./28 This Justice then, and the Seventeen, who are chosen for life, not by vote but by lot, have the absolute right of revising and annulling all sentences passed upon any citizen by other courts, civil or ecclesiastical, or by the king him- self, so that every citizen had the right to summon the king himself before this council. Moreover, they once had the right of electing and deposing the king. But after the lapse of many years the king, Don Pedro, who is called the Dagger, by canvassing,bribery, promises, and every sort of practice, at length procured the revocation of this right. And as soon as he gained his point, he cut of, or, as I would sooner believe, wounded his hand before them all, saying, that not without the loss of royal blood could subjects be allowed to choose their king./29 Yet he effected this change, but upon this condition, "That the subjects have had and shall have the right of taking arms against any violence whatever, whereby any may wish to enter upon the dominion to their hurt, nay, against the king himself, or the prince, his heir, if he thus encroach ." By which condition they certainly rather rectified than abolished that right. For, as we have shown (Chap. IV. Secs. 5, 6), a king can be deprived of the power of ruling, not by the civil law, but by the law of war, in other words the subjects may resist his violence with violence. Besides this condition they stipulated others, which do not concern our present design. Having by these customs given themselves a constitution to the mind of all, they continued for an incredible length of time unharmed, the king's loyalty towards his subjects being as great as theirs towards him. But after that the kingdom fell by inheritance to Ferdinand of Castile, who first had the surname of Catholic; this liberty of the Arragonese began to displease the Castilians, who therefore ceased not to urge Ferdinand to abolish these rights. But he, not yet being accustomed to absolute dominion, dared make no such attempt, but replied thus to his counsellors: that (not to mention that he had received the kingdom of Arragon on those terms, which they knew, and had most solemnly sworn to observe the same, and that it was inhuman to break his word) he was of opinion, that his kingdom would be stable, as long as its safety was as much to the subjects' as to the king's interest, so that neither the king should outweigh the subjects, nor yet the subjects the king; for that if either party were too powerful, the weaker would not only try to recover its former equality, but in vexation at its injury to retaliate upon the other, whence would follow the ruin of either or both. Which very wise language I could not enough wonder at, had it proceeded from a king accustomed to command not freemen but slaves. Accordingly the Arragonese retained their liberties after the time of Ferdinand, though no longer by right but by the favor of their too powerful kings, until the reign of Philip II, who oppressed them with better luck, but no less cruelty, than he did the United Provinces. And although Philip III. is supposed to have restored everything to its former position, yet the Arragonese, partly from eagerness to flatter the powerful (for it is folly to kick against the pricks), partly from terror, have kept nothing but the specious names and empty forms of liberty.

31. We conclude, therefore, that the multitude may preserve under a king an ample enough liberty; if it contrive that the king's power be determined by the sole power, and preserved by the defense of the multitude itself. And this was the single rule which I followed in laying the foundations of monarchy.

CHAPTER VIII.

OF ARISTOCRACY.

So far of monarchy. But now we will say, on what plan an aristocracy is to be framed, so that it may be lasting. 'We have defined an aristocratic dominion as that, which is held not by one man, but by certain persons chosen out of the multitude, whom we shall henceforth call patricians. I say expressly, "that which is held by certain persons chosen." For the chief difference between this and a democracy is, that the right of governing depends in an aristocracy on election only, but in a democracy for the most part on some right either congenital or acquired by fortune (as we shall explain in its place); and therefore, although in any dominion the entire multitude be received into the number of the patricians, provided that right of theirs is not inherited, and does not descend by some law to others, the dominion will for all that be quite an aristocracy, because none are received into the number of the patricians save by express election. But if these chosen persons were but two, each of them will try to be more powerful than the other, and from the too great power of each, the dominion will easily be split into two factions; and in like manner into three, four, or five factions, if three, four, or five persons were put into possession of it. But the factions will be the weaker, the more there are to whom the dominion was delegated. And hence it follows, that to secure the stability of an aristocracy, it is necessary to consider the proportionate size of the actual dominion, in order to determine the minimum number of patricians.

2. Let it be supposed, then, that for a dominion of moderate size it suffices to be allowed a hundred of the best men, and that upon them has been conferred the supreme authority of the dominion, and that they have consequently the right to elect their patrician colleagues, when any of the number die. These men will certainly endeavor to secure their succession to their children or next in blood. And thus the supreme authority of the dominion will always be with those, whom fortune has made children or

kinsmen to patricians. And, as out of a hundred men who rise to office by fortune, hardly three are found that excel in knowledge and counsel, it will thus come to pass, that the authority of the dominion will rest, not with a hundred, but only with two or three who excel by vigor of mind, and who will easily draw to themselves everything, and each of them, as is the wont of human greed, will be able to prepare the way to a monarchy. And so, if we make a right calculation, it is necessary, that the supreme authority of a dominion, whose size requires at least a hundred first-rate men, should be conferred on not less than five thousand. For by this proportion it will never fail, but a hundred shall be found excelling; in mental vigor, that is, on the hypothesis that, out of fifty that seek and obtain office, one will always be found not less than first-rate, besides others that imitate the virtues of the first-rate, and are therefore worthy to rule.

3. The patricians are most commonly citizens of one city, wlhich is the head of the whole dominion, so that the commonwealth or republic has its name from it, as once that of Rome, and now those of Venice, Genoa, etc. But the republic of the Dutch has its name from an entire province, whence it arises, that the subjects of this dominion enjoy a greater liberty. Now, before we can determine the foundations on which this aristocratic dominion ought to rest, we must observe a very great difference, which exists between the dominion which is conferred on one man and that which is conferred on a sufficiently large council. Fur, in the first place, the power of one man is (as we said, Chap. VI. Sec. 5) very inadequate to support the entire dominion; but this no one, without manifest

absurdity, can affirm of a sufficiently large council. For, in declaring the council to be sufficiently large, one at the same time denies, that it is inadequate to support the dominion. A king. therefore, is altogether in need of counsellors, but a council like this is not so in the least. In the second place, kings are mortal, but councils are everlasting. And so the power was of the dominion which has once been transferred to a large enough council never reverts to the multitude. But this is otherwise in a monarchy, as we showed (Chap. VII. Sec. 25). Thirdly, a king's dominion is often on sufferance, whether from his minority, sickness, or old age, or from other causes; but the power of a council of this kind, on the contrary, remains always one and the same. In the fourth place, one man's will is very fluctuating and inconstant; and, therefore, in a monarchy, all law is, indeed, the explicit will of the king (as we said, Chap. VII. Sec. 1), but not every will of the king ought to be law; but this cannot be said of the will of a sufficiently numerous council. For since the council itself, as we have just shown, needs no counsellors, its every explicit will ought to be law. And hence we conclude, that the dominion conferred upon a large enough council is absolute, or approaches nearest to the absolute. For if there be any absolute dominion, it is, in fact, that which is held by an entire multitude.

4. Yet in so far as this aristocratic dominion never (as has just been shown) reverts to the multitude, and there is under it no consultation with the multitude, but, without qualification, every will of the council is law, it must be considered as quite absolute, and therefore its foundations ought to rest only on the will and judgment of the said council, and not on the watchfulness of the

multitude, since the latter is excluded from giving its advice or its vote. The reason, then, why in practice aristocracy is not absolute, is that the multitude is a cause of fear to the rulers, and therefore succeeds in retaining for itself some liberty, which it asserts and holds as its own, if not by an express law, yet on a tacit understanding.

5. And thus it is manifest that this kind of dominion will be in the best possible condition, if its institutions are such that it most nearly approaches the absolute—that is, that the multitude is as little as possible a cause of fear, and retains no liberty, but such as must necessarily be assigned it by the law of the dominion itself, and is therefore not so much a right of the multitude as of the whole dominion, asserted and maintained by the aristocrats only as their own. For thus practice agrees best with theory, as appears from the last section, and is also self-evident.

For we cannot doubt that the dominion rests the less with the patricians, the more rights the commons assert for themselves, such as those which the corporations of artisans in Lower Germany, commonly called Guilds, generally possess.

6. But the commons need not apprehend any danger of a hateful slavery from this form of dominion, merely because it is conferred on the council absolutely. For the will of so large a council cannot be so much determined by lust as by reason; because men are drawn asunder by an evil passion, and cannot be guided, as it were, by one mind, except so far as they desire things honorable, or that have at least an honorable appearance.

7. In determining, then, the foundations of an aristocracy, it is

above all to be observed, that they should rest on the sole will and power of the supreme council, so that it may be as independent as possible, and be in no danger from the multitude. In order to determine these foundations, which are to rest, I say, upon the sole will and power of the council, let us see what foundations of peace are peculiar to monarchy, and unsuited to this form of dominion. For if we substitute for these equivalent foundations fit for an aristocracy, and leave the rest, as they are already laid, we shall have removed without doubt every cause of seditions; or, at least, this kind of dominion will be no less safe than the monarchical, but, on the contrary, so much the more so, and of so much better a condition, as, without danger to peace and liberty, it approaches nearer than monarchy to the absolute (Secs. 3, 6). Fort the greater the right of the supreme authority, the more the form of dominion agrees with the dictate of reason (Chap. III. See. 5/30), and, therefore, the fitter it. is to maintain peace and liberty. Let us run through, the therefore, the points we stated in our sixth chapter, beginning with the ninth section, that we may reject what is unfit for this kind of dominion, and see what agrees with it.

8. That it is necessary, in the first place, to found and fortify one or more cities, no one can doubt. But that city is above all to he fortified, which is the head of the whole dominion, and also those that are on its frontiers. For that which is the head of the whole dominion, and has me supreme right, ought to be more powerful than the rest-. But under this kind of dominion it is quite unnecessary to divide all the inhabitants i11to clans.

9. As for the military, since under this dominion equality is not to

be looked for among all, but between the patricians only, and, in particular, the power of the patricians is greater than that of the commons, it is certain that it makes no difference to the laws or fundamental principles of this dominion, that the military be formed of others besides subjects./31 But it is of the first importance that no one be admitted into the number of the patricians, that has not a proper knowledge of the art of war. But for the subjects to be excluded, as some would have it, from military service, is surely folly. For besides that the military pay given to subjects remains within the realm, whereas, on the contrary, what is paid to a foreign soldiery is altogether lost, the greatest strength of the dominion is also thereby weakened. For it is certain that those fight with peculiar valor who fight for altar and hearth. Whence, also, it is manifest that those are no less wrong, who lay down that military commanders, tribunes, centurions, etc., should be chosen from among the patricians only. For with what courage will these soldiers fight who are deprived of all hope of gaining glory and advancement? But, on the other hand, to establish a law forbidding the patricians to hire foreign soldiers when circumstances require it, whether to defend themselves, and suppress seditions, or for any other reason, besides being inconsiderate, would also be repugnant to the supreme right of the patricians, concerning which see Secs. 3, 4, 5 of this chapter. But the general of a single army, or of the entire military, is to be chosen but in time of war, and among the patricians only, and is to hold the command for a year at most, without power of being continued therein, or afterwards reappointed. For this law, necessary as it is under a monarchy, is so above all under this kind of dominion. For although it is much easier, as we have said above, to transfer the dominion from one man to another than from a free council to one man; yet it does often happen, that patricians are subdued by their own generals, and that to the much greater harm of the commonwealth. For when a monarch is removed, it is but a change of tyrant, not of the form of dominion; but, under an aristocracy, this cannot happen, without an upsetting of the form of dominion, and a slaughter of the greatest men. Of which thing Rome has offered the most mournful examples. But our reason for saying that, under a monarchy, the militia should serve without pay, is here inapplicable. For since the subjects are excluded from giving their advice or votes, they are to be reckoned as foreigners, and are, therefore, to be hired for service on no worse terms than foreigners. And there is in this case no danger of their being distinguished above the rest by the patricians: nay, further, to avoid the partial judgment which everyone is apt to form of his own exploits, it is wiser for the patricians to assign a fixed payment to the soldiers for their service.

10. Furthermore, for this same reason, that all but the patricians are foreigners, it cannot be without danger to the whole dominion, that the lands and houses and the whole soil should remain public property, and be let to the inhabitants at a yearly rent. For the subjects having no part in the dominion would easily, in bad times, all forsake their cities, if they could carry where they pleased what goods they possess. And, therefore, lands and farms are not to be let, but sold to the subjects, yet on condition that they pay every year an aliquot part of the year's

produce, etc., as is done in Holland.

11. These points considered, I proceed to the foundations on which the supreme council should rest and be established. We have shown (Sec. that, in a moderate-sized dominion, this council ought to have about five thousand members. And so we most look for means of preventing the dominion from gradually getting into fewer hands, and of insuring, on the contrary, that the number of members be increased in proportion to the growth of the dominion itself; and, next, that between the patricians, equality be as far as possible maintained; and, further, that there may be speed and expedition in their counsels, and that they tend to the general good; and, lastly, that the power of the patricians or council exceed the power of the multitude, yet so that the multitude suffer no harm thereby.

12. But jealousy causes a great difficulty in maintaining our first point. For men are, as we have said, by nature enemies, so that however they be associated, and bound together by laws, they still retain their nature. And hence I think it is, that democracies change into aristocracies, and these at length into monarchies. For I am fully persuaded that most aristocracies were formerly democracies. For when a given multitude, in search of fresh territories, has found and cultivated them, it retains, as a whole, its equal right of dominion, because no man gives dominion to another spontaneously. But although every one of them thinks it fair, that he should have the same right against another that that other has against him, he yet thinks it unfair, that the foreigners that join them should have equal right in the dominion with themselves, who sought it by their own toil, and won it at the price

of their own blood. And this not even the foreigners themselves deny, for, of course, they migrate thither, not to hold dominion, but for the benefit of their own private business, and are quite satisfied if they are but allowed the liberty of transacting that business in safety. But meanwhile the multitude is augmented by the influx of foreigners, who gradually acquire the national manners, until at last they are distinguished by no other difference than that of incapacity to get office; and while their number daily increases, that of the citizens, on the contrary, is by many causes diminished. For families often die out, and some persons are disqualified for their crimes, and a great many are driven by domestic poverty to neglect affairs of state, and meanwhile the more powerful aim at nothing else, but to govern alone; and thus the dominion is gradually limited to a few, and at length by faction to one. And here we might add other causes that destroy dominions of this sort; but as they are well known, I pass them by, and proceed now to state the laws by which this dominion, of which we are treating, ought to be maintained.

13. The primary law of this dominion ought to be that which determines the proportionate numbers of patricians and multitude. For a proportion (See. 1) ought to be maintained between the multitude and the patricians, so that with the increase of the former the number of the latter should be raised. And this proportion (in accordance with our remarks in the second section) ought to be about fifty to one, that is, the inequality between the members of each should never be greater. For (Sec. 1) without destroying the form of dominion, the number of patricians may be greater than the number of the

multititude. But there is no danger except in the smallness of their number. But how it is to be provided that this law be kept unbroken, I will presently show in its own place.

14. Patricians, in some places, are chosen only out of particular families. But it is ruinous to lay this down expressly by law. For not to mention that families often die out, and that the other families can never be excluded without disgrace, it is also repugnant to the form of this dominion, that the dignity of patrician should be hereditary (See. 1). But on this system a dominion seems rather a democracy, such as we have described in Sec. 1:2, that is in the hands of very few citizens. But, on the other hand, to provide against the patricians choosing their own sons and kinsmen, and thereby against the right of dominion remaining in particular families, is impossible, and indeed absurd, as I shall show (See 39). But provided that they hold that right by no express law, and that the rest (I mean. such as are born within the dominion, and use the vulgar tongue, and have not a foreign wife, and are not infamous, nor servants, nor earning their living by any servile trade, among which are to be reckoned those of a wine-merchant, or brewer) are not excluded, the form of the dominion will, notwithstanding, be retained, and it will be possible to maintain the proportion between the patricians and the multitude.

15. But if it be further by law appointed that no young men be chosen, it will never happen that a few families hold the right of government in their hands. And, therefore, be it by law appointed, that no man that has not reached his thirtieth year be put on the list of candidates.

16. Thirdly, it is next to be ordained, that all the patricians must be assembled at certain fixed times in a particular part of the city, and that whoever does not attend the council, unless he be hindered by illness or some public business, shall be fined some considerable amount. For, were it otherwise, most of them would neglect the public, for the sake of their own private affairs.

17. Let this council's functions be to pass and repeal laws, and to choose their patrician colleagues, and all the ministers of the dominion. For he, that has supreme right, as we have decided that this council has, cannot give to anyone authority to pass and repeal laws, without at the same time abdicating his own right, and transferring it to him, to whom he gives that power. For he, that has but for one day only authority to pass and repeal laws, is able to change the entire form of the dominion. But one can, without forfeiting one's supreme right, temporarily entrust to others the daily business of dominion to be administered according to the established laws. Furthermore, if the ministers of dominion were chosen by any other but this council, then its members would be more properly called wards than patricians.

18. Hence some are accustomed to create for the council a ruler or prince, either for life, as the Venetians, or for a time, as the Genoese; but yet with such great precautions, as make it clear enough, that it is not done without great risk. And assuredly we cannot doubt but that the dominion thereby approaches the monarchical form, and as far as we can conjecture from their histories, it was done for no other reason, than that before the institution of these councils they had lived under a ruler, or doge, as under a king. And so the creation of a ruler is a necessary

requisite indeed for the particular nation, but not for the aristocratic dominion considered in itself.

19. But, inasmuch as the supreme authority of this dominion rests with this council as a whole, not with every individual member of it (for otherwise it would be but the gathering of an undisciplined mob), it is, therefore, necessary that all the patricians be so bound by the laws as to form, as it were, one body governed by one mind. But the laws by themselves alone are Weak and easily broken, when their vindicators are the very persons who are able to transgress them, and the only ones who are to take warning by the punishment, and must punish their colleagues in order by fear of the same punishment to restrain their own desire: for all this involves a great absurdity. And, therefore, means must be sought to preserve order in this supreme council and keep unbroken the constitution of the dominion, so that yet the greatest possible equality may exist between patricians.

20. But since, from a single ruler or prince, able also to vote in the debates, there must necessarily arise a great inequality, especially on account of the power, which must of necessity be granted him, in order to enable him to discharge his duty in safety; therefore, if we consider the whole matter aright, nothing can be devised more useful to the general welfare than the institution of another council of certain patricians subordinate to the supreme council, whose only duty should be to see that the constitution, as far as it concerns the councils and ministers of the dominion be kept unbroken, and who should, therefore, have authority to summon to judgment and, in conformity with established law, to condemn any delinquent who, as a minister of the dominion, has

transgressed the laws concerning his office. And these patricians we shall hereafter call syndics.

21. And they are to be chosen for life. For, were they to be chosen for a time, so that they should afterwards be eligible for other offices in the dominion, we should fall into the very absurdity which we have just pointed out in the nineteenth section. But lest they should become quite haughty by very long rule, none are to be elected to this office, but those who have reached their sixtieth year or more, and have discharged the duties of senator, of which below.

22. Of these, too, we shall easily determine the number, if we consider that these syndics stand to the patricians in the same relation as the whole body of patricians together does to the multitude, which they cannot govern. if they are fewer than a proper number. And, therefore, the number of the syndics should be to that of patricians as their number is to that of the multitude, that is (See. 13), as one to fifty.

23. Moreover, that this council may discharge its functions in security, some portion of the soldiery must be assigned to it, and be subject to its orders.

24. The syndics and other ministers of state are to have no salary, but such emoluments, that they cannot malad-minster affairs of state without great loss to themselves. For we cannot doubt that it is fair, that the ministers of this kind of dominion should be awarded a recompense for their time, since the commons are the majority in this dominion, and the patricians look after their safety, while they themselves have no trouble with affairs of state,

but only with their own private ones. But since, on the other hand, no man (Chap. VII. Sec. 4) defends another's cause, save in so far as he thereby hopes to establish his own interest, things must, of necessity, be so ordered that the ministers, who have charge of affairs of state, should most pursue their own interest, when they are most watch- ful for the general good.

25. To the syndics then, whose duty, as we said, it is to see that the constitution is kept unbroken, the following emoluments are to be awarded: namely, that every householder that inhabits any place in the dominion, be bound to pay every year a coin of small value, say a quarter of an ounce of silver, to the syndics, that thus they may know the number of inhabitants, and so observe what proportion of them the patricians constitute; and next that every new patrician on his election must pay the syndics some large sum, for instance, twenty or twenty-five pounds of silver. Moreover, that money, in which the absent patricians (I mean those who have failed to attend the meeting of the council) are condemned, is also to be awarded to the syndics; and a part, too, of the goods of defaulting ministers, who are bound to abide their judgment, and who are fined a certain sum of money, or have their goods confiscated, should be devoted to them, not to all indeed, but to those only who sit daily, and whose duty it is to summon the council of syndics, concerning whom see Sec. 28. But, in order that the council of syndics may always be maintained at its full number, before all other business in the supreme council, when it is assembled at the usual time, inquiry is to be made about this. "Which, if the syndics neglect, let it then devolve upon the president of the senate (concerning which we shall soon have

occasion to speak), to admonish the supreme council on this head, to demand of the president of the syndics the reason of his silence, and to inquire what is the supreme council's opinion in the matter. But if the president of the senate is likewise silent, let the case be taken up by the president of the supreme court of justice, or if he too is silent by some other patrician, and let him demand an explanation of their silence from the presidents of the senate and the court of justice, as well as from the president of the syndics. Lastly, that that law, where by young men are excluded, may likewise be strictly observed, it is to he appointed that all who have reached the thirtieth year of their age, and who are not by express law excluded, are to have their names inscribed on a list, in presence of the syndics, and to receive from them, at a fixed price, some sign of the honor conferred on them, namely, that they may he allowed to wear a particular ornament only permitted to them, to distinguish them and make them to he had in honor by the rest; and, at the same time, he it ordained, that in elections none may nominate as patrician anyone whose name is not inscribed on the general list, and that under a heavy penalty. And, further, let no one he allowed to refuse the burden of a duty or office, which he is chosen to hear. Lastly, that all the absolutely fundamental laws or the dominion may he everlasting it must he ordained that if anyone in the supreme council raise a question about any fundamental law, as of prolonging the command of any general of an army, or of diminishing the number of patricians, or the like, he is guilty of treason, and not only is he to he condemnedto death. and his goods confiscated, hut some sign of his punishment is to remain visible in public for an eternal memorial of the event. But for the confirming of the other general rights of the do minion, it is enough if it be only ordained, that no law can he repealed nor new law passed, unless first the college of syndics, and then three-fourths or four-fifths of the supreme council agree thereto.

26. Let the right also summing the supreme council and proposing the matters to he decided in it, rest with the syndics, and let them likewise be given the first place in the council, but without the right to vote. But before they take their seats, they must swear by the safety of that supreme council and by the public liberty, that they will strive with the utmost zeal to preserve unbroken the ancient laws. and to consult the general good. After which let them through their secretary open in order the subjects of discussion.

27. But that all the patricians may have equal authority in making decrees and electing the ministers of the dominion, and that speed and expedition in all matters may be possible, the order observed by the Venetians is altogether to be approved, for they appoint by lot a certain number of the council to name the ministers, and when these have named in order the candidates for office, every patrician signifies by ballot his opinion, approving or rejecting the candidate in question, so that it is not afterwards known, who voted in this or that sense. Whereby it is contrived, not only that the authority of all the patricians in the decision is equal, and that business is quickly despatched, but also, that everyone has absolute liberty (which is of the first necessity in councils) to give his opinion without danger of unpopularity.

28. But in the councils of syndics and the other councils, the same order is to be observed, that voting is to be by ballot. But the right of convoking the council of syndics and of proposing the matters to be decided in the same ought to belong to their president, who is to sit every day with ten or more other syndics, to hear the complaints and secret accusations of the commons against the ministers, and to look after the accusers, if circumstances require, and to summon the supreme council even before the appointed time, if any of them judge that there is danger in the delay. Now this president and those who meet with him every day are to be appointed by the supreme council and out of the number of syndics, not indeed for life, but for six months, and they must not have their term renewed but after the lapse of three or four years. And these, as we said above, are to be awarded the goods that are confiscated and the pecuniary fines, or some part of them. The remaining points which concern the syndics we will mention in their proper places.

29. The second council, which is subordinate to the supreme one, we will call the senate, and let its duty be to transact public business, for instance, to publish the laws of the dominion, to order the fortifications of the cities according to law, to confer military commissions, to impose taxes on the subjects and apply the same, to answer foreign embassies, and decide where embassies are to be sent. But let the actual appointment of ambassadors be the duty of the supreme council. For it is of the greatest consequence to see that no patrician be called to any oflice in the dominion but by the supreme council itself, lest the patricians themselves should try to curry favor with the senate.

Secondly, all matters are to be referred to the supreme council, which in any way alter the existing state of things, as the deciding on peace and war. Wherefore, that the Senate's decrees concerning peace and war may be valid, they must be confirmed by the supreme council. And therefore I should say, that it belonged to the supreme council only, not to the senate, to impose new taxes.

30. In determining the number of senators these points are to be taken into consideration: first, that all the patricians should have an equal hope of gaining senatorial rank; secondly, that notwithstanding the same senators, whose time (for which they were elected) is elapsed, may be continued after a short interval, that so the dominion may always be governed by skilled and experienced men; and lastly, that among the senators many may be found illustrious for wisdom and virtue. But to secure all these conditions, there can be no other means devised, than that it should be by law appointed, that no one who has not reached his fiftieth year, be received into the number of senators, and that four hundred, that is about a twelfth part of the patricians, be appointed for a year, and that two years after that year has elapsed, the same be capable of re-appointment. For in this manner about a twelfth part of the patricians will be constantly engaged in the duty of senator, with only short intervening periods; and this number surely, together with that made up by the syndics, will be little less than the number of patricians that have attained their fiftieth year. And so all the patricians will always have a great hope of gaining the rank of senator or syndic, and yet notwithstanding, the same patricians, at only short intervals, will always hold

senatorial rank, and (according to What we said, See. 2) there will never be wanting in the senate distinguished men, ex- celling in counsel and skill. And because this law cannot be broken without exciting great jealousy on the part of many patricians, it needs no other safeguard for its constant validity, than that every patrician who has reached the age we mentioned, should offer the proof thereof to the syndics, who shall put his name on the list of candidates for the senatorial duties, and read the name before the supreme council, so that he may occupy, with the rest of the same rank, a place set apart in this supreme council for his fellows, next to the place of the senators.

31. The emoluments of the senators should be of such a kind, that their profit is greater from peace than from war. And therefore let there be awarded to them a hundredth or a fiftieth part of the merchandise exported abroad from the dominion, or imported into it from abroad. For we cannot doubt, that by this means they will, as far as they call, preserve peace, and never desire to protract war. And from this duty not even the senators themselves, if any of them are merchants, ought to be exempt; for such an immunity cannot be granted without great risk to trade, as I think no one is ignorant. Nay, on the contrary, it must be by law ordained, that no senator or ex-senator may fill any military post; and further, that no one may be declared general or praetor, which officers we said (See. 9) were to be only appointed in time of war, whose father or grandfather is a senator, or has held the dignity of senator within two years. Which laws we cannot doubt, that the patricians outside the senate will defend with all their might: and so it will be the case, that the senators will always have more profit from

peace than from war, and will, therefore, never advise war, except the utmost need of the dominion compels them. But it may be objected to us, that on this system, if, that is, syndics and senators are to be allowed so great profits, an aristocracy will be as burdensome to the subjects as any monarchy. But not to mention that royal courts require larger expenditure, and are yet not provided in order to secure peace, and that peace can never be bought too dear; it is to be added, first, that all that under a monarchy is conferred on one or a few, is here conferred upon very many. Next kings and their ministers do not bear the burden of the dominion with the subjects, but under this form, of dominion it is just the reverse; for the patricians, who are always chosen from the rich, bear the largest share of the weight of the commonwealth. Lastly, the burdens of a monarchy spring not so much from its king's expenditure, as from its secret policy. For those burdens of a dominion, that are imposed on the citizens in order to secure peace and liberty, great though they be, are yet supported and lightened by the usefulness of peace. What nation ever had to pay so many and so heavy taxes as the Dutch? Yet it not only has not been exhausted, but, on the contrary, has been so mighty by its wealth, that all envied its good fortune. If therefore the burdens of a monarchy were imposed for the sake of peace, they would not oppress the citizens; but, as I have said, it is from the secret policy of that sort of dominion, that the subjects faint under their lord; that is, because the virtue of kings counts for more in time of war than in time of peace, and because they, who would reign by themselves, ought above all to try and have their subjects poor; not to mention other things, which that most prudent Dutchman V. H./32 formerly remarked, because they do not concern my design, which is only to describe the best state of every kind of dominion.

32. Of the syndics chosen by the supreme council, some should sit in the senate, but without the right of voting, so that they may see whether the laws concerning that assembly be duly observed, and may have the supreme council convoked, when anything is to be referred to it from the senate. For the supreme right of convoking this council, and proposing to it subjects of discussion, is, as we have already said, with the syndics. But before the votes of the contemporaries of the senators be taken, the president of the senate for the time being shall explain the state of affairs, and what the senate's own opinion is on the matter in question, and why; after which the votes shall be collected in the accustomed order.

33. The entire senate ought not to meet every day, but, like all great councils, at a certain fixed time. But as in the mean time the business of the dominion must be executed, it is, therefore, necessary that some part of the senators be chosen, who, on the dismissal of the senate, shall supply its place, and whose duty it shall be to summon the senate itself, when need is; to execute its orders about affairs of state; to read letters written to the senate and supreme council; and, lastly, to consult about the matters to be proposed in the senate. But that all these points, and the order of this assembly, as a whole, may be more easily conceived, I will describe the whole matter more precisely.

34:. The senators who, as we have said already, are to be chosen for a year, are to be divided into four or six series, of which let the first have the first seat in the senate for the first three or two months in the year; and at the expiration of this time, let the second series take the place of the first, and so on, observing their turns, so that that series which was first in the first months may be last in the second period. Furthermore, there are to be appointed as many presidents as there are series, and the same number of vice-presidents to fill their places when required——that is, two are to be chosen out of every series, one to be its president, the other its vice-president. And let the president of the first series preside in the senate also, for the first months; or, in his absence, let his vice-president fill his place; and so on with the rest, observing the same order as above. Next, out of the first series, some are to be chosen by vote or lot to fill the place of the senate, when it is dismissed, in conjunction with the president and vice-president of the same series; and that, for the same space of time, as the said series occupies the first place in the senate; and thus, when that time is past, as many are again to be chosen out of the second series, by vote or lot, to fill, in conjunction with their president and vice-president, the place of the first series, and supply the lack of a senate; and so on with the rest. And there is no need that the election of these men—I mean those that I have said are. to be chosen for periods of three or two months, by vote or lot——should be made by the supreme council. For the reason which we gave in the twenty-ninth section is not here applicable, much less the reason stated in the seventeen. It suffices, then, that they be elected by the senate and the syndics present at its meeting.

35. But of these persons we cannot so precisely ascertain the number. However, this is certain, that they must be too numerous to be easily susceptible of corruption. For though they can by themselves determine nothing concerning aflairs of state, yet they can delay the senate, or, what would be worst of all, delude it by putting forward matters of no importance, and keeping back those that are of greater—not to mention that, if they were too few, the absence of one or two might delay public business. But as, on the contrary, these consuls are for that very reason appointed, because great councils cannot devote themselves every day to public business, a remedy must be looked for necessarily here, and their inadequacy of number be made up for by the shortness of their term of office. And thus, if only thirteen or so be chosen for two or three months, they will be too many to be corrupted in this short period. And for this cause, also, did I recommend that their successors should by no means be appointed. except at the very time when they do succeed, and the others go away.

36. We have said, that it is also their duty, when any, though few, of them think it needful, to convoke the senate, to put. before it the matters to be decided, to dismiss it, and to execute its orders about public business. But I will now briefly state the order in which this ought to be done, so that business may not be long protracted by useless questions. Let, then, the consuls consult about the matter to be proposed in the senate, and what is required to be done; and, if they are all of one mind about it, then let them convoke the senate, and, having duly explained the question, let them set forth what their opinion is, and, without waiting for another's opinion, collect the votes in their order. But

if the consuls support more than one opinion, then, in the senate, that opinion is first to be stated on the question proposed, which was supported by the larger number of consuls. And if the same is not approved by the majority of senate and consuls, but the waverers and opponents together are in a majority, which is to be determined by ballot, as we have already mentioned, then let them set forth the second opinion, which had fewer votes than the former among the consuls, and so on with the rest. But if none be approved by a majority of the whole senate, the senate is to be adjourned to the next day, or for a short time, that the consuls meanwhile may see, if they can find other means, that may give more satisfaction. But if they do not succeed in finding other means, or if the majority of the senate refuses to approve such as they have found, then the opinion of every senator is to be heard; and if the majority of the senate also refuses to support any of these, then the votes are to be taken again on every opinion, and not only the affirmative votes, as hitherto, but the doubtful and negative are to be counted. And if the affirmative prove more numerous than the doubtful or negative, then that opinion is to hold good; but, on the contrary, to be lost, if the negative prove more numerous than the doubtful or affirmative. But if on every opinion there is a greater number of doubters than of voters for and against, then let the council of syndics join the senate, and vote with the senators, with only affirmative and negative votes, omitting those that signify a hesitating mind. And the same order is to be observed about matters referred by the senate to the supreme council. So much for the senate.

37. As for the court of justice or bench, it cannot rest upon the

same foundations as that which exists under a. monarch, as we described it in Chap. VI. Secs. 26, and following. For (Sec. 14) it agrees not with the foundations of our present dominion, that any account he made of families or clans. And there must be a further difference, because judges chosen from the patricians only might indeed be restrained by the fear of their patrician successors, from pronouncing any unjust judgment against any of the patricians, and, perhaps, would hardly have the courage to punish them after their deserts; but they would, on the other hand, dare everything against the commons, and daily carry off the rich among them for a prey. I know that the plan of the Genoese is therefore approved by many, for they choose their judges not among the patricians, but among foreigners. But this seems to me, considering the matter in the abstract, absurdly ordained, that foreigners and not patricians should he called in to interpret the laws. For what are judges but interpreters of the laws'? And I am therefore persuaded that herein also the Genoese have had regard rather to the genius of their own race, than to the very nature of this kind of dominion. We most, therefore, by considering the matter in the abstract, devise the means which best agree with the form of this government.

38. But as far as regards the number of the judges, the theory of this constitution requires no peculiar number; but as under monarchical dominion, so under this, it suffices that they be too numerous to be corrupted by a private man. For their duty is but to provide against one private person doing wrong to another, and therefore to decide disputes between private persons, as well patricians as commons, and to exact penalties from delinquents,

and even from patricians, syndics, and senators, as far as they have offended against the laws, whereby all are bound. But disputes that may arise between cities that are subject to the dominion, are to be decided in the supreme coubcil.

39. Furthermore the principle regulating the time, for which the judges should be appointed, is the same in both dominions, and also the principle of a certain part of them retiring every year; and, lastly, although it is not necessary for every one of them to be of a different family, yet it is necessary that two related by blood should not sit on the same bench together. And this last point is to be observed also in the other councils, except the supreme one, in which it is enough, if it be only provided by law that in elections no man may nominate a relation, nor vote upon his nomination by another, and also that two relations may not draw lots from the urn for the nomination of any minister of the dominion. This, I say, is sufficient in a council that is composed of so large a number of men, and has no special profits assigned to it. And so utterly un-harmed will the dominion be in this quarter, that it is absurd to pass a law excluding from the supreme council the relations of all the patricians, as we said in the four- tenth section. But that it is absurd is manifest. For that law could not be instituted by the patricians themselves, without their thereby all absolutely abdicating their own right, and therefore not the patricians themselves but the commons would defend this law, which is directly contrary to what we proved in Secs. 5 and 6. But that law of the dominion, whereby it is ordained that the same uniform proportion be maintained between the numbers of the patricians and the multitude, chiefly contemplates this end of preserving the

patricians' right and power, that is, provides against their becoming too few to be able to govern the multitude.

40. But the judges are to be chosen by the supreme council out of the patricians only, that is (See. 17) out of the actual authors of the laws, and the judgments they pass, as well in civil as criminal cases, shall be valid, if they were pronounced in due course of justice and without partiality; into which matter the syndics shall be by law authorized to inquire, and to judge and determine thereof.

41. The judges' emoluments ought to be the same, as we mentioned in the twenty-ninth section of the sixth chapter; namely, that they receive from the losing party upon every judgment which they pass in civil cases, an aliquot part of the whole sum at stake. But as to their sentences in criminal cases, let there be here this difference only, that the goods which they confiscate, and every fine whereby lesser crimes are punished, be assigned to themselves only, yet on this condition, that they may never compel anyone to confess by torture, and thus, precaution enough will be taken against their being unfair to the commons, and through fear too lenient to the patricians. For besides that this fear is tempered by avarice itself, and that veiled under the specious name of justice, they are also numerous, and vote, not openly, but by ballot, so that a man may be indignant at losing his case, but can have no reason to impute it to a particular person. Moreover the fear of the syndics will restrain them from pronouncing an inequitable, or at least absurd sentence, or from acting any of them treacherously, besides that in so large a number of judges there will always be one or two, that the unfair

stand in awe of. Lastly, as far as the commons are concerned, they also will be adequately secured if they are allowed to appeal to the syndics, who, as I have said, are by law authorized to inquire, judge, and determine about the conduct of the judges. For it is certain that the syndics will not be able to escape the hatred of the patricians, and on the other hand, will always be most popular with the commons, whose applause they will try as far as they can to bid for. To which end, opportunity being given them, they will not fail to reverse sentences pronounced against the laws of the court, and to examine any judge, and to punish those that are partial, for nothing moves the hearts of a multitude more than this. Nor is it an objection, but, on the contrary, an advantage, that such examples can but rarely occur. For not to mention that that commonwealth is ill ordered where examples are daily made of criminals (as we showed Chap. V. See. 2), those events must surely be very rare that are most renowned by fame.

42. Those who are sent as governors to cities and provinces ought to be chosen out of the rank of senators, because it is the duty of senators to look after the fortifications of cities, the treasury, the military, etc. But those, who were sent to somewhat distant regions, would be unable to attend the senate, and, therefore, those only are to be summoned from the senate itself, who are destined to cities founded on their native soil; but those whom they wish to send to places more remote are to he chosen out of those, whose age is consistent with senatorial rank. But not even thus do I think that the peace of the dominion will be sufficiently provided for, that is, if the neighboring cities are altogether denied the right of vote, unless they are so weak, that they can be

openly set at naught, which cannot surely be supposed. And so it is necessary, that the neighboring cities lie granted the right of citizenship, and that from every one of them twenty, or thirty. or forty chosen citizens (for the number should vary with the size of the city) be enrolled among the patricians, out of whom three, four, or five ought to be yearly elected to be of the senate, and one for life to be a syndic. And let those who are of the senate be sent with their syndic, to govern the city out of which they were chosen.

43. Moreover, judges are to be established in every city, chosen out of the patricians of that city. But of these I think it unnecessary to treat at length, because they concern not the foundations of this sort of dominion in particular.

44. In every council the secretaries and other officials of this kind, as they have not the right of voting, should be chosen from the commons. But as these, by their long practice of business, are the most conversant with the affairs to be transacted, it often arises that more deference than right is shown to their advice, and that the state of the whole dominion depends chiefly on their guidance: which thing has been fatal to the Dutch. For this cannot happen without exciting the jealousy of many of the noblest. And surely we cannot doubt, that a senate, whose wisdom is derived from the advice, not of senators, but of officials, will be most frequented by the sluggish, and the condition of this sort of dominion will be little better than that of a monarchy directed by a few counsellors of the king. (See Chap. VI. Secs. 5-7). However, to this evil the dominion will be more or less liable, according as it was well or ill founded. For the liberty of a dominion is never

defended without risk, if it has not firm enough foundations; and, to avoid that risk, patricians choose from the commons ambitious ministers, who are slaughtered as victims to appease the wrath of those, who are plotting against liberty. But where liberty has firm enough foundations, there the patricians themselves vie for the honor of defending it, and are anxious that prudence in the conduct of affairs should flow from their own advice only; and in laying the foundations of this dominion we have studied above all these two points, namely, to exclude the commons from giving advice as much as from giving votes (Secs. 3, 4:), and, therefore, to place the whole authority of the dominion with the whole body of patricians, but its exercise with the syndics and senate, and, lastly, the right of convoking the senate, and treating of matters affecting the common welfare with consuls chosen from the senate itself. But, if it is further ordained that the secretary, whether in the senate or in other councils, be appointed for four or five years at most, and have attached to him an assistant-secretary appointed for the same period, to bear part of the work during that time, or that the senate have not one, but several secretaries, employed one in one department, and another in another, the power of the officials will never become of any consequence.

45. Treasurers are likewise to be chosen from the commons, and are to be bound to submit the treasury accounts to the syndics as well as to the senate.

46. Matters concerning religion we have set forth at sufficient length in our Theologico-Political Treatise. Yet certain points we then omitted, of which it was not there the place to treat; for

instance, that all the patricians must be of the same religion, that is, of that most simple and general religion, which in that treatise we described. For it is above all to be avoided, that the patricians themselves should be divided into sects, and show favor, some to this, and others to that, and thence become mastered by superstition, and try to deprive the subjects of the liberty of speaking out their opinions. In the second place, though everyone is to be given liberty to speak out his opinion, yet. great conventicles are to be forbidden. And, therefore, those that are attached to another religion are, indeed, to be allowed to build as many temples as they please; yet these are to be small, and limited to a certain standard of size, and on sites at some little distance one from another. But it is very important, that the temples consecrated to the national religion should be large and costly, and that only patricians or senators should be allowed to ad- minister its principal rites, and thus that patricians only be allowed to baptize, celebrate marriages, and lay on hands, and that in general they be recognized as the priests of the temples and the champions and interpreters of the national religion. But, for preaching. and to manage the church treasury and its daily business, let some persons be chosen from the commons by the senate itself. to be, as it were, the senate's deputies, and, there- fore, bound to render it account of everything.

47. And these are points that concern the foundations of this sort of dominion; to which I will add some few others less essential indeed, but yet of great importance. Namely, that the patricians, when they walk, should be distinguished by some special garment, or dress, and be saluted by some special title; and that

every man of the commons should give way to them; and that, if any patrician has lost his property by some unavoidable misfortune, he should be restored to his old condition at the public expense; but if, on the contrary, it be proved that he has spent the same in presents, ostentation, gaming, debauchery, &e., or that he is insolvent, he must lose his dignity, and be held unworthy of every honor and office. For he, that cannot govern himself and his own private affairs, will much less be able to advise on public affairs.

48. Those, whom the law compels to take an oath, will be much more cautious of perjury, if they are bidden to swear by the country's safety and liberty and by the supreme council, than if they are told to swear by God. For he who swears by God, gives as surety some private advantage to himself, whereof he is judge; but he, who by his oath gives as surety his country's liberty and safety, swears by what is the common advantage of all, whereof he is not judge, and if he perjures himself, thereby de- clares that he is his country's enemy.

49. Academies, that are founded at the public expense, are instituted not so much to cultivate men's natural abilities as to restrain them. But in a free commonwealth arts and sciences will be best cultivated to the full, if everyone that asks leave is allowed to teach publicly, and that at his own cost and risk. But these and the like points I reserve for another place./33 For here I determined to treat only such matters as concern an aristocratic dominion only.

CHAXPTER IX.

OF ARISTOCRACY. CONTINUATION.

Hithereo We have considered an aristocracy, so far as it takes its name from one city, which is the head of the whole dominion. It is now time to treat of that, which is in the hands of more than one city, and which I think preferable to the former. But that we may notice its difference and its superiority, we will pass in review the foundations of dominion, one by one, rejecting those foundations, which are unsuited to the present kind, and laying in their place others for it to rest upon.

2. The cities, then, which enjoy the right of citizenship, must be so built and fortified, that, on the one hand, each city by itself may be unable to subsist without; the rest, and that yet, on the other hand, it cannot desert the rest without great harm to the whole dominion. For thus they will always remain united. But cities, which are so constituted, that they can neither maintain themselves, nor be dangerous to the rest, are clearly not independent, but absolutely subject to the rest.

3. But the contents of the ninth and tenth sections of the last chapter are deduced from the general nature of aristocracy as are also the proportion between the numbers of patricians the multitude and the proper age and condition of those that are to e made patricians: so that on these points no difference can arise. whether the dominion be in the hands of one or more cities. But; the supreme council most here be on a different footing. For it any city of the dominion were assigned for the meeting of this supreme council, it would in reality be the head of the dominion ; and, the therefore, either they would have to take turns, or a place

would have to be assigned for this council, that has not the right of citizenship, and belongs equally to all. But either alternative is as difficult to effect, as it is easy to state; I mean, either that so many thousands of men should have to go often outside their cities, or that they should have to assemble sometimes in one place, sometimes in another.

4. But that we may conclude aright what should be done in this matter, and on1 what plan the councils of this dominion ought to be formed, from its own very nature and condition, these points are to be considered; namely, that every city has so much more right than a private man, as it excels him in power (Chap. II. See. 4), and consequently that every city of this dominion has as much right within its walls, or the limits of its jurisdiction, as it has power; and, in the next place, that all the cities are mutually associated and united, not as under a treaty, but as forming one dominion, yet so that every city has so much more right as against the dominion than the others, as it exceeds the others in power. For he who seeks equality between unequals, seeks an absurdity. Citizens, indeed, are rightly esteemed equal, because the power of each, compared with that of the whole dominion, is of no account. But each city's power constitutes a large part of the power of the dominion itself, and so much the larger, as the city itself is greater. And, therefore, the cities cannot all be held equal. But, as the power of each, so also its right should be estimated by its greatness. The bonds, however, by which they should be bound into one dominion, are above all a senate and a court of justice (Chap. IV. Sec. 1). But how by these bonds they are all to be so united, that each of them may yet remain, as far as possible,

independent, I will here briefly show.

51. suppose then, that the patricians of every city, who, according to its size, should be more, or fewer (See. 3), have supreme right over their own city, and that, in that city's supreme council, they have supreme authority to fortify the city and enlarge its walls, to impose taxes, to pass and repeal laws, and, in general, to do everything which they judge necessary to their city's preservation and increase. But to manage the common business of the dominion, a senate is to be created on just the same footing as we described in the last chapter, so that there be between this senate and the former no difference, except that this has also authority to decide the disputes, which may arise between cities. For in this dominion, of which no city is head, it cannot be done by the supreme council. (See Chap. VI. Sec. 38.)

6. But, in this dominion, the supreme council is not to be called together, unless there is need to alter the form of the dominion itself, or on some difficult business, to which the senators shall think themselves unequal; and so it will very rarely happen, that all the patricians are summoned to council. For we have said (Chap. VH1. Sec. 17), that the supreme council's function is to pass and repeal laws, and to choose the ministers of the dominion. But the laws, or general constitution of the whole dominion, ought not to be changed as soon as instituted. If, however, time and occasion suggest the institution of some new law or the change of one already ordained, the question may first be discussed in the senate, and after the agreement of the senate in the matter, then let envoys next be sent to the cities by the senate itself, to inform the patricians of every city of the opinion

of the senate, and lastly, if the majority of the cities follow that opinion, it shall then remain good, but otherwise be of no effect. And this same order may be observed in choosing the generals of the army and the ambassadors to be sent to other realms, as also all out decrees concerning; the making of war or accepting conditions of peace. But in choosing the other public officials, since (as we showed in Sec. -1) every city, as far as can be ought to remain independent, and to have as much more right than the others in the dominion, as it exceeds them in power, the following order must necessarily be observed. The senators are to be chosen by the patricians of each city; that is, the patricians of one city are to elect in their own council a fixed number of senators from their colleagues of their own city. which number is to be to that of the patricians of that city as one to twelve (Chap. VIII. bee. 30); and they are to designate whom they will to be of the first, second, third, or other series; and in like number the patricians of the other cities, in proportion to their. number, are to choose more or fewer senators, and distribute them among the series, into a certain number of which we have said the senate is to be divided. (Chap. VIII. Sec. 34:.) By which means it will result, that in every series of senators there will be found senators of every city, more or fewer, according to its size. But the presidents and vice-presidents of the series, being fewer in number than the cities, are to be chosen by lot by the senate out of the consuls, who are to be appointed first. The same order is to be maintained in appointing the supreme judges of the dominion, namely, that the patricians of every city are to elect from their colleagues in proportion to their number more or fewer judges. And so it will be the case, that every city in choosing officials will be as independent as possible, and that each, in proportion to its power, will have the more right alike in the senate and the court of justice; supposing, that is, that the order observed by senate and court in deciding public affairs, and settling disputes is such in all respects, as we have described it in the thirty-third and thirty-fourth sections of the last chapter./34

7. Next, the commanders of battalions and military tribunes are also to be chosen from the patricians. For as it is fair, that every city in proportion to its size should be bound to levy a certain number of soldiers for the general safety of the whole dominion, it is also fair, that from the patricians of every city in proportion to the number of regiments, which they are bound to maintain, they may appoint so many tribunes, captains, ensigns, etc., as are needed to discipline that part of the military, which they supply to the dominion.

8. No taxes are to be imposed by the senate on the subjects; but to meet the expenditure, which by decree of the senate is necessary to carry on public business, not the subjects, but the cities themselves are to be called to assessment by the senate, so that every city, in proportion to its size, should pay a larger or smaller share of the expense. And this share indeed is to be exacted by the patricians of every city from their own citizens in what way they please, either by compelling them to an assessment, or, as is much fairer, by imposing taxes on them.

9. Further, although all tl1e cities of this dominion are not maritime, nor the senators summoned from the maritime cities

only, yet may the same emoluments be awarded to the senators, as we mentioned in the thirty-first section of the last chapter. To which end it will he posible to devise means, varying with the composition of the dominion, to link the cities to one another more closely. But the other points concerning the senate and the court of justice and the whole dominion in general, which I delivered in the last chapter, are to be applied to this dominion also. And so we see, that in a dominion which is in the hands of several cities, it will not he necessary to assign a fixed time or place for assembling the supreme council. But for the senate and court of justice a place is to he appointed in a village, or in a city, that has not the right of voting. But I return to those points, which concern the cities taken by themselves.

10. The order to be observed by the supreme council of a single city, in choosing officials of the dominion and of the city. and in making decrees, should be the same that I have delivered in the twenty-seventh and thirty-six sections of the last chapter. For the policy is the same here as it was there. Next a council of syndics is to he formed, subordinate to the council of the city, and having, the same relation to it as the council of syndics of the last chapter had to the council of the entire dominion. and let its functions within the limits of the city be also the same, and let it enjoy the same emoluments. But if a city, and consequently the number of its patricians be so small that it cannot create more than one syndic or two, which two are not enough to make a council, then the supreme council of the city is to appoint judges to assist. the syndics in trials according to the matter at issue, or else the dispute must he referred to the supreme council of syndics. For

from every city some also out of the syndics are to be sent to the place where the senate sits, to see that the constitution of the whole dominion is preserved unbroken, and they are to sit in the senate without the right of voting.

11. The consuls of the cities are likewise to be chosen by the patricians of their city, and are to constitute a sort of senate for it. But their number I cannot determine, nor yet do I think it necessary, since the city's business of great importance is transacted by its supreme council, and matters concerning the whole dominion by the great senate. But if they be few, it will be necessary that they give their votes in their council openly, and not by ballot, as in large councils. For in small councils, when votes are given secretly, by a little extra cunning one can easily detect the author of every vote, and in many ways deceive the less attentive.

12. Besides, in every city judges are to be appointed by its supreme council, from whose sentence, however, let everyone but an openly convicted criminal or confessed debtor have a right of appeal to the supreme court of justice of the dominion. But this need not be pursued further.

13. It remains, therefore, to speak of the cities which are not independent. If these were founded in an actual province or district of the dominion, and their inhabitants are of the same nation and language, they ought of necessity, like villages, to be esteemed parts of the neighboring cities, so that each of them should be under the government of this or that independent city. And the reason of this is, that the patricians are chosen by the

supreme council, not of the dominion, but of every city, and in every city are more or fewer, according to the number of inhabitants within the limits of its jurisdiction (See. 5). And so it is necessary, that the multitude of the city, which is not independent, be referred to the census of another which is independent, and depend upon the latter's government. But cities captured by right of war, and annexed to the dominion, are either to be esteemed associates in the dominion, and though conquered put under an obligation by that benefit, or else colonies to enjoy the right of citizenship are to be sent thither, and the natives removed elsewhere or utterly destroyed,

14. And these are the things, which touch the foundations of the dominion. But that its condition is better than that of the aristocracy, which is called after one city only, I conclude from this, namely, that the patricians of every city, after the manner of human desire, will be eager to keep, and if possible increase their right, both in their city and in the senate; and therefore will try, as far as possible, to attract the multitude to themselves, and consequently to make a stir in the dominion by good deeds rather than by fear, and to increase their own number; because the more numerous they are, the more senators they will choose out of their own council (See. 6), and hence the more right (Sec. 6) they will possess in the dominion. Nor is it an objection, that while every city is consulting its own interest and suspecting the rest, they more often quarrel among themselves, and waste time in disputing. For if, while the Romans are debating, Saguntum is lost:/35 on the other hand, while a few are deciding everything in conformity with their own passions only, liberty and the general

good are lost. For men's natural abilities are too dull to see through everything at once; but by consulting, listening, and debating, they grow more acute, and while they are trying all means, they at last discover those which they want, which all approve, but no one would have thought of in the first instance. But if anyone retorts, that the dominion of the'Dutch has not long endured without a count or one to fill his place, let him have this reply, that the Dutch thought, that to maintain their liberty it was enough to abandon their count, and to behead the body of their dominion, but never thought of remolding it, and left its limbs, just as they had been first constituted, so that the county of Holland has remained without a count, like a headless body, and the actual dominion has lasted on without the name. And so it is no wonder that most of its subjects have not known, with whom the authority of the dominion lay. And even had this been otherwise, yet those who actually held dominion were far too few to govern the multitude and suppress their power- ful adversaries. Whence it has come to pass, that the latter have often been able to plot against them with impunity, and at last to overthrow them. And so the sudden overthrow of the said republic/3 has not arisen from a useless waste of time in debates, but from the misformed state of the said dominion and the fewness of its rulers.

15. This aristocracy in the hands of several cities is also preferable to the other, because it is not necessary, as in the first described, to provide against its whole supreme council being overpowered by a sudden attack, since (Sec. 9) no time or place is appointed for its meeting. Moreover, powerful citizens in this dominion are less

to be feared. For where several cities enjoy liberty, it is not enough for him, who is making ready his way to dominion, to seize one city, in order to hold dominion over the rest. And, lastly, liberty under this dominion is common to more. For where one city reigns alone, there the advantage of the rest is only so far considered, as suits that reigning city.

CHAPTER X.

OF ARISTOCRACY. CONCLUSION.

Having explained and made proof of the foundations of both kinds of aristocracy, it remains to inquire whether by reason of any fault they are liable to be dissolved or changed into another form. The primary cause, by which dominions of this kind are dissolved, is that, which that most acute Florentine/37 observes in his Discourses on Livy (Bk. iii. Chap. I.), namely, that like a human body, "a dominion has daily added to it something that at some time or other needs to be remedied." And so, he says, it is necessary for something occasionally to occur, to bring back the dominion to that first principle, on which it was in the beguining established. And if this does not take place within the necessary time, its blemishes will go on increasing. till they cannot be removed, but with the dominion itself. And this restoration, he says, may either happen accidentally or by the design and forethought of the laws or of a man of extraordinary virtue. And we cannot doubt. that this matter is of the greatest importance, and that, where provision has not been made against this inconvenience, the dominion will not be able to endure by its own excellence, but only by good fortune; and on the other hand that, where a proper remedy has been applied to this evil, it will not be possible for it to fall by its own fault, but only by some inevitable fate, as we shall presently show more clearly. The first remedy, that suggested itself for this evil, was to appoint every five years a supreme dictator for one or two months, who should have the right to inquire, decide, and make ordinances concerning the acts of the senators and of every official, and thereby to bring back the dominion to its first principle. But he who studies to avoid the inconveniences, to which a dominion is liable, must apply remedies that suit its nature, and can be derived from its own foundations; otherwise in his wish to avoid Charybdis he falls upon Scylla. It is, indeed, true that all, as well rulers as ruled, ought to be restrained by fear of punishment or loss, so that they may not do wrong with impunity or even advantage; but, on the other hand, it is certain, that if this fear becomes common to good and bad men alike, the dominion must be in the utmost danger. Now as the authority of a dictator is absolute, it cannot fail to be a terror to all, especially if, as is here required, he were appointed at a stated time, because in that case every ambitious man would pursue this office with the utmost energy; and it is certain that in time of peace virtue is thought less of than wealth, so that the more haughty a man he is, the more easily he will get office. And this perhaps is why the Romans used to make a dictator at no fixed time, but under pressure of some accidental necessity. Though for all that, to quote Cicero's words, "the tumor of a dictator was displeasing to the good."/38 And to be sure, as this authority of a dictator is quite royal, it is impossible for the dominion to change into a monarchy without great peril to the republic, although it happen for ever so short a time. Furthermore, if no fixed time were appointed for creating a dictator, no notice would be paid to the interval between one dictator and another, which is the very thing that we said was most to be observed; and the whole thing would be exceedingly vague, and therefore easily neglected. Unless, then, this authority of a dictator be eternal and fixed, and therefore impossible to be conferred on one man without destroying the form of dominion, the dictatorial authority itself, and consequently the safety and preservation of the republic will be very uncertain.

2. But, on the other hand, we cannot doubt (Chap. VI. Sec. 3), that, if without destroying the form of dominion, the sword of the dictator might be permanent, and only terrible to the wicked, evils will never grow to such a pitch, that they cannot be eradicated or amended. In order, therefore, to secure all these conditions, we have said, that there is to he a council of syndics subordinate to the supreme council, to the end that the sword of the dictator should be permanent in the hands not of any natural person, but of a civil person, whose members are too numerous to divide the dominion amongst themselves (Chap. IX. Secs. 1, 2, or to combine in any wickedness. To which is to he added, that they are forbidden to fill any other office in the dominion, that they are not the paymasters of the soldiery, and, lastly, that they are of an age to prefer actual security to things new and perilous. Wherefore the dominion is in no danger from them, and consequently they cannot, and in fact will not he a terror to the good, but only to the wicked. For as they are less powerful to accomplish criminal designs, so are they more so to restrain

wickedness. For, not to mention that they can resist it in its beginnings (since the council lasts for ever), they are also sufficiently numerous to dare to accuse and condemn this or that influential man without fear of his enmity; especially as they vote by ballot, and the sentence is pronounced in the name of the entire council.

3. But the tribunes of the commons at Rome were likewise regularly appointed; but they were too weak to restrain the power of a Scipio, and had besides to submit to the senate their plans for the public welfare,/39 which also frequently eluded them, by contriving that the one whom the senators were least afraid of should he most popular with the commons. Besides which, the tribunes' authority was supported against the patricians by the favor of the commons, and whenever they convoked the commons, it looked as if they were raising a sedition rather than ascending a council. Which inconveniences have certainly no place in the dominion which we have described in the last two chapter

4-. However, this authority of the syndics will only be able to secure the preservation of the form of the dominion, and thus to prevent the laws from being broken, or anyone from gaining by transgressing; but will by no means suflice to prevent the growth of vices, which cannot be forbidden by law, such as those into which men fall from excess of leisure, and from which the ruin of a dominion not uncommonly follows. For men in time of peace lay aside fear, and gradually from being fierce savages become civilized or humane, and from being humane become soft and sluggish, and seek to excel one another not in virtue, but in ostentation and luxury. And hence they begin to put off their native manners and to put on foreign ones, that is, to become slaves.

5. To avoid these evils many have tried to establish sumptuary laws; but in vain. For all laws which can be broken without any injury to another, are counted but a laughing-stock, and are so far from bridling the desires and lusts of men, that on the contrary they stimulate them. For "we are ever eager for forbidden fruit, and desire what is denied."/40 Nor do idle men ever lack ability to elude the laws which are instituted about things, which cannot absolutely be forbidden, as banquets, plays, ornaments, and the like, of which only the excess is bad; and that is to be judged according to the individual's fortune, so that it cannot be determined by any general law.

6. I conclude, therefore, that the common vices of peace, of which we are here speaking, are never to be directly, but indirectly forbidden; that is, by laying such foundations of dominion, that the result may be, that the majority, I do not say are anxious to live wisely (for that is impossible), but are guided by those passions whence the republic has most advantage. And therefore the chief point to be studied is, that the rich may be, if not thrifty, yet avaricious. For there is no doubt, that, if this passion of avarice, which is general and lasting, be encouraged by the desire of glory, most people would set their chief affection upon increasing their property without disgrace, in order to acquire honors, while avoiding extreme infamy. If then we examine the foundations of both kinds of aristocracy which I have explained in the last two chapters, we shall see, that this very result follows from them. For

the number of rulers in both is so large, that most of the rich have access to government and to the offices of the dominion open to them.

7. But if it be further ordained (as we said, Chap. VIII. Se ,. 47), that patricians who are insolvent be deposed from patrician rank, and that those who have lost their property by misfortune be restored to their former position, there is no doubt that all will try their best to keep their property. Moreover, they will never desire foreign costumes, nor disdain their native ones, if it is by law appointed, that patricians and candidates for office should be distinguished by a special robe, concerning which see Chap. VIII. Sees. 25, 47. And besides these, other means may be devised in every dominion agreeable to the nature of its situation and the national genius, and herein it is above all to be studied, that the subjects may do their duty rather spontaneously than under pressure of the law.

8. For a dominion, that looks no farther than to lead men by fear, will be rather free from vices, than possessed of virtue. But men are so to be led, that they may think that they are not led, but living after their own mind, and according; to their free decision; and so that they are restrained only by love of liberty, desire to increase their property, and hope of gaining the honors of the dominion. But effigies, triumphs, and other incitements to virtue. are signs rather of slavery than liberty. For rewards of virtue are granted to slaves, not freemen. I admit, indeed, that men are very much stimulated by these incitements; but, as in the first instance, they are awarded to great men, so afterwards, with the growth of envy, they are granted to cowards and men swollen with the extent of their wealth, to the great indignation of all good men. Secondly,

those, who boast of their ancestors' effigies and triumphs, think they are wronged if they are not preferred to others. Lastly, not to mention other objections, it is certain that equality which once cast off the general liberty is lost, can by no means be maintained, from the time that peculiar honors by public law decreed to any man renowned for his virtue.

9. After which premisses, let us now see whether dominions of this kind can be destroyed by any cause to which blame attaches. But if any dominion can be everlasting, that will necessarily be so, whose constitution being once rightly instituted remains unbroken. For the constitution is the soul of a dominion. Therefore, if it is preserved, so is the dominion. But a constitution cannot remain unconquered, unless it is defended alike by reason and common human passion: otherwise, if it relies only on the help of reason, it is certainly weak and easily overcome. Now since the fundamental constitution of both kinds of aristocracy has been shown to agree with reason and common human passion, we can therefore assert that these, if any kinds of dominion, will be eternal, in other words, that they cannot be destroyed by any cause to which blame attaches, but only by some inevitable fate.

10. But it may still be objected to us, that, although the constitution of dominion above set forth is defended by reason and common human passion, yet for all that it may at some time be overpowered. For there is no passion, that is not sometimes overpowered by a stronger contrary one; for we frequently see the fear of death overpowered by the greed for another's property. Men, who are running away in panic fear from the enemy, can be stopped by the fear of nothing else, but throw themselves into

rivers, or rush into fire, to escape the enemy's steel. In whatever degree, therefore, a commonwealth is rightly ordered, and its laws well made; yet in the extreme difficulties of a dominion, when all, as sometimes happens, are seized by a sort of panic terror, all, without regard to the future or the laws, approve only that which their actual fear suggests, all turn towards the man who is renowned for his victories, and set him free from the laws, and (establishing thereby the worst of precedents), continue him in command, and entrust to his fidelity all affairs of state: and this was, in fact, the cause of the destruction of the Roman dominion, But to answer this objection, I say, first, that in a rightly constituted republic such terror does not arise but from a due cause. And so such terror and consequent confusion ca be attributed to no cause avoidable by human foresight. In the next place, it is to be observed, that in a republic such as we have above described, it is impossible (Chap. VIII. Secs. 9, 25) for this or that man so to distinguish himself by the report of his virtue, as to turn towards himself the attention of all, but he must have many rivals favored by others. And so, although from terror there arise some confusion in the republic, yet no one will be able to elude the law and declare the election of anyone to an illegal military command, without its being immediately disputed by other candidates; and to settle the dispute, it will, in the end, be necessary to have recourse to the constitution ordained once for all, and approved by all, and to order the affairs of the dominion according to the existing laws. I may therefore absolutely assert, that as the aristocracy, which is in the hands of one city only, so especially that which is in the hands of several, is everlasting, or, in other words, can be dissolved or changed into another form by no internal cause.

CHAPTER XI.

OF DEMOCRACY.

I pass, at length, to the third and perfectly absolute dominion, which we call democracy. The difference between this and aristocracy consists, we have said, chieffly in this, that in an aristocracy it depends on the supreme council's will and free choice only, that this or that man is made a patrician, so that no one has the right to vote or fill public offices by inheritance, and that no one can by right demand this right, as is the case in the dominion, whereof we are now treating. For all, who are born of citizen parents, or on the soil of the country, or who have deserved well of the republic, or have accomplished any other conditions upon which the law grants to a man right of citizenship; they all, I say, have a right to demand for themselves the right to vote in the supreme council and to fill public offices, nor can they be refused it, but for crime or infamy.

2. If, then, it is by a law appointed, that the elder men only, who have reached a certain year of their age, or the first born only, as soon as their age allows, or those who contribute to the republic a certain sum of money, shall have the right of voting in the supreme council and managing the business of the dominion; then, although on this system the result might be, that the supreme council would be composed of fewer citizens than that of the aristocracy of which we treated above, yet, for all that, dominions of this kind should be called democracies, because in

them the citizens, who are destined to manage affairs of state, are not chosen as the best by the supreme council, but are destined to it by a law. And although for this reason dominions of this kind, that is, where not the best, but those who happen by chance to be rich, or who are born eldest, are destined to govern, are thought inferior to an aristocracy; yet, if we reflect on the practice or general condition of mankind, the result in both cases will come to the same thing. For patricians will always think those the best, who are rich, or related to themselves in blood, or allied by friendship. And, indeed, if such were the nature of patricians, that they were free from all passion, and guided by mere zeal for the public welfare in choosing their patrician colleagues, no dominion could be compared with aristocracy. But experience itself teaches us only too well, that things pass in quite a contrary manner, above all, in oligarchies, Where the will of the patricians, from the absence of rivals, is most free from the law. For there the patricians intentionally keep away the best men from the council, and seek for themselves such colleagues in it, as hang upon their words, so that in such a dominion things are in a much more unhappy condition, because the choice of patricians depends entirely upon the arbitrary will of a few, which is free or unrestrained by any law. But I return to my subject.

3. From what has been said in the last section, it is manifest that we can conceive of various kinds of democracy. But my intention is not to treat of every kind, but of that only, "wherein all, without exception, who owe allegiance to the laws of the country only, and are further independent and of respectable life, have the right of voting in the supreme council and of filling the ofiices of the

dominion." I say expressly. "who owe allegiance to the laws of the country only," to exclude foreigners, who are treated as being under another's dominion. I added, besides, "who are independent," except in so far as they are under allegiance to the laws of the dominion, to exclude women and slaves, who are under the authority of men and masters, and also children and wards, as long as they are under the authority of parents and guardians. I said, lastly, "and of respectable life," to exclude, above all, those that are infamous from crime, or some disgraceful means of livelihood.

4. But, perhaps, someone will ask, whether women are under men's authority by nature or institution? For if it has been by mere institution, then we had no reason compelling us to exclude women from government. But if we consult experience itself, we shall find that the origin of it is in their weakness. For there has never been a case of men and women reigning together, but wherever on the earth men are found, there we see that men rule, and women are ruled, and that on this plan, both sexes live in harmony. But on the other hand, the Amazons, who are reported to have held rule of old, did not suffer men to stop in their country, but reared only their female children, killing the males to whom they gave birth./41 But if by nature women were equal to men, and were equally distinguished by force of character and ability, in which human power and therefore human right chiefly consist; surely among nations so many and different some would be found, where both sexes rule alike, and others, where men are ruled by women, and so brought up, that they can make less use of their abilities. And since this is nowhere the case, one may

assert with perfect propriety, that women have not by nature equal right with men: but that they necessarily give way to men, and that thus it cannot happen, that both sexes should rule alike, much less that men should be ruled by women. But if we further reflect upon human passions, how men, in fact, generally love women merely from the passion of lust, and esteem their cleverness and wisdom in proportion to the excellence of their beauty, and also how very ill-disposed men are to suffer the women they love to show any sort of favor to others, and other facts of this kind, we shall easily see that men and women cannot rule alike without great hurt to peace. But of this enough.

NOTES:

1 Ethics, iv. 4, Coroll. iii. 31, note; 32, note.

2. ibid., v. 42, note.

3. Theologico-Political Treatise, Chap. xvi.

4. Ethics, iv. 37, note 2.

5. Ibid., ii. 48, 49, note.

6. Virgil, Ecl. ii, 65

7. Romans ix. 21.

8. Literally, "oil and trouble "——a common proverbial expression in Latin.

9. Justin, Histories, xxxii. iv.

10. In his book called Il Principe, or The Prince.

11. Curtius, 3;.

12. Daniel vi. 15.

13. Hom. "Odys.," xii.

14. Chap. I. See. 4 of the speech, or rather letter, which is not now admitted to be a genuine work of Sallust.

15. Ethics, iii. 29, &c.

16. This seems to he a mistake for See. 4, "majori suhditorum parti utile erit. «qual in hoe coneilio plurimo haberit suffragia." " What has most votes in such in. council, will be to the interest of the greater part of the subjects."

17. Sam. xv. :51.

18. Taeitus:, Histories, i., 7.

19. Antonio Perez, a publicist, and professor of law in the University Latvan in the first part of the seventeenth century.

20. Chap. VI. Sec. 10.

21. Chap VI, Secs 11, 15,16.

22. Chap. VI. Secs. 27, 28.

23. Chap. VI. Sec. 31.

24. Chap. VI. Sec. 36.

25. 1 Kings xiv. 25 3 2 Chron. xii.

26. The war between France and Spain, terminated by the first peace of Aix-la-Chapelle, 1665.

27. Chap. VI. Sec. 37.

28. See Hallam's History of the Middle Ages, Chap. IV., for the constitutional history of Arragon. Hallam calls the Justiza the Justiciary, but the literal translation, Justice, seems warranted by our own English use of the word to designate certain judges.

29. Hallam says, that the king merely cut the obnoxious Privilege of Union, which he describes rather differently, through with his sword. The Privilege of Union was so utterly "eradicated from the records of the kingdom, that its precise words have never been recovered."

30. Ought not this reference to be to Chap. III. Sec. 6 ?

31. Cf. Chap. VI. Sec. 10.

32. "This V. II. is Pieter de la Court (1618-85). an ex: inept publicist, who wrote under the initials D. C. (De la la Court), V. H. (Van den lhove, the Dutch equivalent). He was a. Friend of John de Witt, and opposed to the party of the Statholders."——Pollock's Life and Philosophy of Spinoza, towards end of Chap. X.

33. This promise is not kept by the author, no doubt owing to his not living to finish the work.

34. So the text: but the court of justice is not described till the thirty- seventh and following sections of Chap. VIII

35. Livy, "Hist.," Bk. xxi. Chaps. VI. and following.

36. A.D. 1672. William Henry, Prince of Orange, afterwards Willian III. of England, was made Statholder by a popular insurrection, consequent on the invasion of the French.

37. Machiavelli.

38. Cic. ad Quint. Grat. iii. 8, 4. The better reading is "rumor," not "tumor." "The good" in such a passage means the aristocratic party.

39. Not by law, except before n.c. 297 and in the interval between the dictatorship of Sulla and the eonsulship of Pompey and Crassus. But in the golden age of the republic the senate in fact controlled the tribunes.

40. Ovid, Amores, III. iv. 17.

41. Justin, Histories, ii. 4.

ANNEX

CHAPTER XX.

THAT IN A FREE STATE EVERY MAN MAY THINK WHAT HE LIKES, AND SAY WHAT HE THINKS.

If men's minds were as easily controlled as their tongues, every king would sit safely on his throne, and government by compulsion would cease; for every subject would shape his life according to the intentions of his rulers, and would esteem a thing true or false, good or evil, just or unjust, in obedience to their dictates. However, We have shown already (Chapter XVII.) that no man's mind can possibly lie wholly at the disposition of another, for no one can willingly transfer his natural right of free reason and judgment, or be compelled so to do. For this reason government which attempts to control minds is accounted tyrannical, and it is considered an abuse of sovereignty and a usurpation of the rights of subjects, to seek to prescribe what shall be accepted as true, or rejected as false, or what opinions should actuate men in their worship of God. All these questions fall within a man's natural right, which he cannot abdicate even with his own consent.

I admit that the judgment can be biassed in many ways, and to an almost incredible degree, so that while exempt from direct external control it may be so dependent on another man's words, that it may fitly be said to be ruled by him; but although this influence is carried to great lengths, it has never gone so far as to invalidate the statement, that every man's understanding is his own, and that brains are as diverse as palates.

Moses, not by fraud, but by Divine virtue, gained such a hold over the popular judgment that he was accounted superhuman, and believed to speak and act through the inspiration of the Deity; nevertheless, even he could not escape murmurs and evil interpretations. How much less then can other monarchs avoid them! Yet such unlimited power, if it exists at all, must belong to a monarch, and least of all to a democracy, where the whole or a great part of the people wield authority collectively. This is a fact which I think everyone can explain for himself.

However unlimited, therefore, the power of a sovereign may be, however implicitly it is trusted as the exponent of law and religion, it can never prevent men from forming judgments according to their intellect, or being influenced by any given emotion. It is true that it has the right to treat as enemies all men whose opinions do not, on all subjects, entirely coincide with its own; but we are not dismissing its strict rights, but its proper course of action. I grant that it has the right to rule in the most violent manner, and to put citizens to death for very trivial causes, but no one supposes it can do this with the approval of sound judgment. Nay, inasmuch as such things cannot be done without extreme peril to itself, we may even deny that it has the absolute power to do them, or, consequently, the absolute right; for the rights of the sovereign are limited by his power.

Since, therefore, no one can abdicate his freedom of judgment and feeling; since every man is by indefeasible natural right the master of his own thoughts, it follows that men thinking in diverse and contradictory fashions, cannot, without disastrous results, be compelled to speak only according to the dictates of the supreme power. Not even the most experienced, to say nothing of the multitude, know how to keep silence. Men's common failing is to confide their plans to others, though there be need for secrecy, so that a government would be most harsh which deprived the individual of his freedom of saying and teaching what he thought; and would be moderate if such freedom were granted. Still we cannot deny that authority may be as much injured by words as by actions; hence, although the freedom we are discussing cannot be entirely denied to subjects, its unlimited concession would be most baneful; we must, therefore, now inquire, how far such freedom can and ought to be conceded without danger to the peace of the state, or the power of the rulers; and this. as I. said at the beginning of Chapter XVI., is my principal object.

It. follows, plainly, from the explanation given above, of the foundations of a state. that the ultimate aim of government is not to rule, or restrain, by fear, nor to exact obedience, but contrariwise, to free every man from fear, that he may live in all possible security; in other words, to strengthen his natural right to exist and work without injury to himself or others. .

No, the object of government is not to change men from rational beings into beasts or puppets, but to enable them to develop their minds and bodies in security, and to employ their reason unshackled; neither showing hatred, anger, or deceit, nor watched with the eyes of jealousy and injustice. In fact, the true aim of government is liberty.

Now we have seen that in forming a state the power of making laws must either be vested in the body of the citizens, or in a portion of them, or in one man. For, although men's free judgments are very diverse, each one thinking that he alone knows everything, and although complete unanimity of feeling and speech is out of the question, it is impossible to preserve peace, unless individuals abdicate their right of acting entirely on their own judgment. Therefore, the individual justly cedes the right of free action, though not of free reason and judgment; no one can act against the authorities without danger to the state, though his feelings and judgment may be at variance therewith; he may even speak against them, provided that he does so from rational conviction, not from fraud, anger, or hatred, and provided that he does not attempt to introduce any change on his private authority.

For instance, supposing a man shows that a law is repugnant to sound reason, and should therefore be repealed; if he submits his opinion to the judgment of the authorities (who, alone, have the right of making and repealing laws), and meanwhile acts in nowise contrary to that law, he has deserved well of the state, and has behaved as a good citizen should; but if he accuses the authorities of injustice, and stirs up the people against them, or if he seditiously strives to abrogate the law without their consent, he is a mere agitator and rebel.

Thus we see how an individual may declare and teach what he

believes, without injury to the authority of his rulers, or to the public peace; namely, by leaving in their hands the entire power of legislation as it affects action, and by doing nothing against their laws, though he be compelled often to act in contradiction to what he believes, and openly feels, to be best.

Such a course can be taken without detriment to justice and dutifulness, nay, it is the one which a just and dutiful man would adopt. We have shown that justice is dependent on the laws of the authorities, so that no one who contravenes their accepted decrees can be just, while the highest regard for duty, as we have pointed out in the preceding chapter, is exercised in maintaining public peace and tranquillity; these could not be preserved if every man were to live as he pleased; therefore it is no less than undutiful for a man to act contrary to his country's laws, for if the practice became universal the ruin of states would necessarily follow.

Hence, so long as a man acts in obedience to the laws of his rulers, he in nowise contravenes his reason, for in obedience to reason he transferred the right of controlling his actions from his own hands to theirs. This doctrine we can confirm from actual custom, for in a conference of great and small powers, schemes are seldom carried unanimously, yet all unite in carrying out what is decided on, whether they voted for or against. But I return to my proposition.

From the fundamental notions of a state, we have discovered how a man may exercise free judgment without detriment to the supreme power: from the same premises we can no less easily determine what opinions would be seditious. Evidently those which by their very nature nullify the compact by which the right of free action was ceded. For instance, a man who holds that the supreme power has no rights over him, or that promises ought not to be kept, or that everyone should live as he pleases, or other doctrines of this nature in direct opposition to the above-mentioned contract, is seditious, not so much from his actual opinions and judgment, as from the deeds which they involve; for he who maintains such theories abrogates the contract which tacitly, or openly, he made with his rulers. Other opinions which do not involve acts violating the contract, such as revenge, anger, and the like, are not seditious, unless it be in some corrupt state, where superstitious and ambitious persons, unable to endure men of learning, are so popular with the multitude that their word is more valued than the law.

However, I do not deny that there are some doctrines which, while they are apparently only concerned with abstract truths and falsehoods, are yet propounded and published with unworthy motives. This question we have discussed in Chapter XV., and shown that reason should nevertheless remain unshackled. If we hold to the principle that a man's loyalty to the state should be judged, like his loyalty to God, from his actions only—namely, from his charity towards his neighbors; we cannot doubt that the best government will allow freedom of philosophical speculation no less than of religious belief. I confess that from such freedom inconveniences may sometimes arise, but what question was ever settled so wisely that no abuses could possibly spring therefrom? He who seeks to regulate everything by law, is more likely to arouse vices than to reform them. It is best to grant what cannot be abolished, even though it be in itself harmful. How many evils spring from luxury, envy, avarice, drunkenness, and the like, yet these are tolerated——vices as they are——because they cannot be prevented by legal enactments. How much more then should free thought be granted, seeing that it is in itself a virtue and that it cannot be crushed! Besides, the evil results can easily be checked, as I will show, by the secular authorities, not to mention that such freedom is absolutely necessary for progress in science and the liberal arts: for no man follows such pursuits to advantage unless his judgment be entirely free and unhampered.

But let it be granted that freedom may be crushed, and men be so bound down, that they do not dare to utter a whisper, save at the bidding of their rulers; nevertheless this can never be carried to the pitch of making them think according to authority, so that the necessary consequences would be that men would daily be thinking one thing and saying another, to the corruption of good faith, that mainstay of government, and to the fostering of hateful flattery and perfidy, whence spring stratagems, and the corruption of every good art.

It is far from possible to impose uniformity of speech, for the more rulers strive to curtail freedom of speech, the more obstinately are they resisted; not indeed by the avaricious, the flatterers, and other numskulls, who think supreme salvation consists in filling their stomachs and gloating over their money-bags, but by those whom good education, sound morality, and virtue have rendered more free. Men, as generally constituted, are most prone to resent the branding as criminal of opinions which they believe to be true, and the prescription as wicked of that which inspires them with piety towards God and man; hence they are ready to forswear the laws and conspire against the authorities, thinking it not shameful but honorable to stir up seditions and perpetuate any sort of crime with this end in view. Such being the constitution of human nature, we see that laws directed against opinions affect the generous-minded rather than the wicked, and are adapted less for coercing criminals than for irritating the upright; so that they cannot be maintained without great peril to the state.

Moreover, such laws are almost always useless, for those who hold that the opinions proscribed are sound, cannot possibly obey the law; whereas those who already reject them as false, accept the law as a kind of privilege, and make such boast of it, that authority is powerless to repeal it, even if such a course be subsequently desired.

To these considerations may be added what we said in Chapter XVIII. in treating of the history of the Hebrews. And, lastly, how many schisms have arisen in the Church from the attempt of the authorities to decide by law the intricacies of theological controversy! If men were not allured by the hope of getting the law and the authorities on their side, of triumphing over their adversaries in the sight of an applauding multitude, and of acquiring honorable distinctions, they would not strive so maliciously, nor would such fury sway their minds. This is taught not only by reason but by daily examples, for laws of this kind pre-scribing what every man shall believe and forbidding anyone to speak or write to the contrary, have often been passed, as sops or concessions to the anger of those who cannot tolerate men of enlightenment, and who, by such harsh and crooked enactments, can easily turn the devotion of the masses into fury and direct it against whom they will.

How much better would it be to restrain popular anger and fury, instead of passing useless laws, which can only be broken by those who love virtue and the liberal arts, thus paring down the state till it is too small to harbor men of talent. What greater misfortune for a state can be conceived than that honorable men should be sent like criminals into exile, because they hold diverse opinions which they cannot disguise? What, I say, can be more hurtful than that men who have committed no crime or wickedness should, simply because they are enlightened, be treated as enemies and put to death, and that the scaffold, the terror of evil-doers, should become the arena where the highest examples of tolerance and virtue are displayed to the people with all the marks of ignominy that' authority can devise?

He that knows himself to be upright does not fear the death of a criminal, and shrinks from no punishment; his mind is not wrung with remorse for any disgraceful deed: he holds that death in a good cause is no punishment, but an honor, and that death for freedom is glory.

What purpose then is served by the death of such men, what example is proclaimed? the cause for which they die is unknown to the idle and the foolish, hateful to the turbulent, loved by the upright. The only lesson we can draw from such scenes is to flatter the persecutor, or else to imitate the victim.

If formal assent is not to be esteemed above conviction, and if governments are to retain a firm hold of authority and not be compelled to yield to agitators, it is imperative that freedom of judgment should be granted, so that men may live together in harmony, however diverse, or even openly contradictory their opinions may be. We cannot doubt that such is the best system of government and open to the fewest objections, since it is the one most in harmony with human nature. In a democracy (the most natural form of government, as we have shown in Chapter XVI.) everyone submits to the control of authority over his actions, but not over his judgment and reason; that is, seeing that all cannot think alike, the voice of the majority has the force of law, subject to repeal if circumstances bring about a change of opinion. In proportion as the power of free judgment is withheld we depart from the natural condition of mankind, and consequently the government becomes more tyrannical.

In order to prove that from such freedom no inconvenience arises, which cannot easily be checked by the exercise of the sovereign power, and that men's actions can easily be kept in bounds, though their opinions be at open variance, it will be well to cite an example. Such an one is not very far to seek. The city of Amsterdam reaps the fruit of this freedom in its own great prosperity and in the admiration of all other people. For in this most flourishing state, and most splendid city, men of every nation and religion live together in the greatest harmony, and ask no questions before trusting their goods to a fellow-citizen, save whether he be rich or poor, and whether he generally acts honestly, or the reverse. His religion and sect is considered of no importance: for it has no effect before the judges in gaining or losing a cause, and there is no sect so despised that its followers, provided that they harm no one, pay every man his due, and live uprightly, are deprived of the protection of the magisterial authority.

On the other hand, when the religious controversy between Remonstrants and Counter-Remonstrants began to be taken up by politicians and the States, it grew into a schism, and abundantly showed that laws dealing with religion and seeking to settle its controversies are much more calculated to irritate than to reform, and that they give rise to extreme license: further, it was seen that schisms do not originate in a love of truth, which is a source of courtesy and gentleness, but rather in an inordinate desire for supremacy, From all these considerations it is clearer than the sun at noonday, that the true schismatics are those who condemn other men's writings, and seditiously stir up the quarrelsome masses against their authors, rather than those authors themselves, who generally write only for the learned, and appeal solely to reason. In fact, the real disturbers of the peace are those who, in a free state, seek to curtail the liberty of judgment which they are unable to tyrannize over.

I have thus shown:

I). That it is impossible to deprive men of the liberty of saying what they think.

II). That such liberty can be conceded to every man without injury to the rights and authority of the sovereign power, and that every man may retain it without injury to such rights, provided that he does not presume upon it to the extent of introducing any new rights into the state, or acting in any way contrary to the existing laws.

III). That every man may enjoy this liberty without detriment to the public peace, and that no inconveniences arise therefrom which cannot easily be checked.

IV). That every man may enjoy it without injury to his allegiance.

V). That laws dealing With speculative problems are entirely useless. VI). Lastly, that not only may such liberty be granted without prejudice to the public peace, to loyalty, and to the rights of rulers, but that it is even necessary for their preservation. For when people try to take it away, and bring to trial, not only the acts which alone are capable of offending, but also the opinions of mankind, they only succeed in surrounding their victims with an appearance of martyrdom, and raise feelings of pity and revenge rather than of terror. Uprightness and good faith are thus corrupted, flatterers and traitors are encouraged, and sectarians triumph, inasmuch as concessions have been made to their animosity, and they have gained the state sanction for the doctrines of which they are the interpreters. Hence they arrogate to themselves the state authority and rights, and do not scruple to assert that they have been directly chosen by God, and that their laws are Divine, whereas the laws of the state are human, and should therefore yield obedience to the laws of God——in other words, to their own laws. Everyone must see that this is not a state of afiairs conducive to public welfare. wherefore, as we have shown in Chapter XVIII, the safest way for a state is to lay down the rule that religion is comprised solely in the exercise of charity and justice, and that the rights of rulers in sacred, no less than in secular matters, should merely have to do with actions, but that every man should think what he likes and say what he thinks.

I have thus fulfilled the task I set myself in this treatise. It remains only to call attention to the fact that I have written nothing which I do not most willingly submit to the examination and approval of my country's rulers; and that I am willing to retract anything which they shall decide to be repugnant to the laws, or prejudicial to the public good. I know that I am a man, and as a man liable to error, but against error I have taken scrupulous care, and have striven to keep in entire accordance with the laws of my country, with loyalty, and with morality.

. . . .

www.ingramcontent.com/pod-product-compliance
Lightning Source LLC
Chambersburg PA
CBHW022109280326
41933CB00007B/308